IN MEMORY OF HENRY C. ALTER

Special thanks to Richard Freeman for encouraging me to keep writing, and to Kiki for helping me fly again.

I WAS FOR SALE.
By Lisa B. Falour

Published by Green Candy Press
www.greencandypress.com

Copyright © 2001 Lisa B. Falour

First published in the U.K. in 2000 by Velvet Publications

Cover and interior design: Todd Simmons
Cover photograph: Larry Utley
Cover model: Shelley

Printed in Canada by Transcontinental Printing, Inc.

Lisa B. Falour is American. She received a B.S. degree from Hunter College, City University of New York in 1982, and an M.B.A. degree from Baruch College, City University of New York, in 1989. She also attended or was enrolled at Kent State University in Ohio, Antioch College in Ohio, Brooklyn College in New York, and the University of Florence, Italy. Formally trained as a graphic artist, Lisa self-published two "zines" for many years, MODERN GIRLZ and BIKINI GIRL. Her artwork is in the permanent collections of many museums around the world and she has also been active in film, video and music projects. Her writing was first published around 1975. Since then, she has written for TEENAGE RAMPAGE, THE EAST VILLAGE EYE, OP, IMPULSE, THE AMERI-CAN BOOK REVIEW, UNGAWA!, WET, BLACK ICE, BATTERIES NOT INCLUDED, and GREY AREAS, to name only a few. Her writing has appeared in at least five literary anthologies, among them: MONDO BARBIE (St. Martin's Press, 1993) UNBEARABLES (AutoNoMedia/Semiotext(e), 1995) BEST OF TEMP SLAVE! (Garrett County Press, 1997) BLACK ICE (University of Colorado, 1998), and GUILTY PLEASURES (Masquerade Books, 1999). Lisa began her bondage modeling career in 1978 in New York City and has only recently retired. "Those ball gags are just too hard on my dental work," she says.

introduction

postscript

I started writing when I was about eight years old — little mystery stories, about two pages long. I would have written longer stories, but I ran out of energy very quickly.

My mother was the person who encouraged me to write. She also advised me to keep diaries, which I have done for most of my life. I have a huge collection of dusty journals dating back to the 1960s, and I find it difficult to read them. They are just too painful to look at. When I see what a good little girl I was, so full of optimism and fascination with life, it tears at my heart. At 41, my spirit is broken, I am alcoholic, and my bouts of depression are now lasting years at a time. I wish I could meet the little girl I was and sit and have a long talk with her about all the ugly things she was going to see in the world. I wish, so passionately, I could have had some means to see into my future, so that I could have avoided some of the terrible, terrible mistakes I have made.

But we all wish that, don't we? And of course, such things are not possible, unless we have very good astrologers. I met two good ones. The first told me I would self-destruct. The second told me it was very important for me to write about my experiences with the dark, hidden and dirty side of life I would encounter. I feel almost certain I will not live to see the publication of this book. I also feel very certain that telling the things I tell in this book will have some sort of positive social impact, somewhere. At least, I hope they will. So I guess both astrologers were right. I wish I could feel happier about my destiny, but instead I can only pour another glass of wine to try to stop my hands from shaking.

My real name is Lisa B. Falour. Of course, I am incredibly fearful about revealing my true identity, but I also feel it is very important not to hide behind pseudonyms. I am sure my family, the few friends I have left, and my past and future employers will take a negative view of this book project. I certainly do. It's ugly. It's not good writing, either, not that I ever claimed to be a good writer. I have been involved in a lot of sick, strange things in my life and am absolutely compelled to tell about them. Not to brag and not to titillate, but to try to save young people from making the mistakes I did, and to get older people to think about why foolish souls like myself fall into sin.

Most of the people I've met in my dirty little voyages have been driven to their acts of self-degradation for one of two reasons: no self-respect; and/or economic necessity. As time goes by and I am more and more beaten down by the trials of daily existence, I believe more and more firmly that each person who turns a blind eye to ugly realities they'd rather not face is sinning in one of the worst ways possible. And yet, to be a crusader for "good" is to let yourself in for nothing but trouble.

So, what to do? Don't ask me. If I had the answers, I would-
n't be sitting here in this poorly lit room in suburban Paris, France,
unwashed and essentially unemployable, spending much of my
spare time reading true crime books and considering the most efficient methods of committing suicide. If it makes you feel better to
point your finger at me and say, "She's fucked up," I suggest you
go and wash that finger, because chances are it's very dirty, indeed.

I was born in 1957 in Ohio, U.S.A. I don't know very much
about my family except that I may be related by marriage to inven-
tor Charles Kettering. I guess not knowing much about one's family is extremely American. Our "history" doesn't go back very far,
does it? I don't have an accurate memory, myself, but mine is a
long one and goes back to before the time I knew how to walk or
talk. My parents said a lot of things around me I am sure they did-
n't think I could understand, and hearing these things gave me a
rather twisted outlook on life. My parents were fairly cold and crit-
ical toward me, so I failed to bond with them, and also I have very
low self-esteem. My parents are surely not, however, completely to
blame for my deep-seated failure to be able to see wrong from
right. I have a dark side, which I believe would often prevail no
matter in which circumstances I had been raised. When I was
about seven or eight years old, my parents gave me a child's record
player, and when my mother's mother was "babysitting" me (her
version of which was to drink Scotch, smoke Chesterfields and
watch television, and leave me to my own devices as long as I did-

n't break anything around the apartment), she turned a blind eye on my habit of raiding my father's record collection. My favorite song was by Eartha Kitt: "I Wanna Be Evil" I memorized the words and would dance around the bedroom I shared with my little brother, and would dream of growing up and running off and doing bad things. My Grandma would haul her big ass out of the chair in front of the "telly", as she called it (no, she was not British, she was Slovenian) and come back into the bedroom and watch me dance around and sing and would cheer me on. Then, she'd light up another Chesterfield, top up her cocktail, chuckle very, very happily, and shuffle back off to look at the "telly" some more. (She loved Westerns.) When my parents got home, I'd have the Eartha record put back in its place and pretend to be very occupied with my Barbie doll, and Grandma would say I had been a perfect angel. If my parents had bothered to look closely, they would have seen that I enjoyed dressing up my Barbie doll as a slut.

As far as I can recall, I wasn't sexually abused as a child, though I probably would have enjoyed that. I did get a lot of slaps in the face from my Mom, which I definitely didn't enjoy. I had lots of little friends in the neighborhood, both boys and girls. For reasons not clear to me, we all often played very rough role-playing games and I was usually cast as the victim. For example, when we'd play "Tarzan", I was invariably the "helpless white woman lost in the jungle", which meant that my little male friends could spring up behind me, throw me to the ground and straddle me, pretending to tear off my clothes and rape me, although none of us had a very clear idea of how rape was exactly achieved, since we didn't know anything specific about sex at that age. Another good game was "Roy Rogers" For us, it was a chance to strap on toy cowboy pistols and tie each other up, except I was the one who seemed to get tied up the most. I really enjoyed it, too. One day, my little friends tied me up very securely and left me there and forgot about me. I gleefully struggled out of my bonds, although I couldn't figure out how to get the toy handcuffs off my wrists. I had a little cowgirl outfit complete with embroidered felt cowgirl hat, and ran up the driveway, laughing, my hands still cuffed. My Grandma was there in the back yard, and at first looked alarmed that I was in partial bondage, but when she saw how much I was enjoying it, she just laughed and went back inside to her "telly."

Violent games continued to be a part of my childhood. There was a television series at the time called "Combat!" and the Catholic family with four kids who lived downstairs from us, the McKees, simply adored this program. I would often watch it with them, and felt very shocked at the images of the poor, dirty soldiers behind barbed wire, but the McKee kids had a huge collection of plastic "army men" and would set up elaborate war scenarios in their parents' dining room and make extremely impressive noises imitating bombs, hand grenades and machine guns, as they "killed" each other. They assured me war was wonderful, and the most honorable part about it was getting "wounded." I quickly developed a fantasy I'd play in my head at night after lights out, in which I was a male soldier, getting "wounded." I imagined myself falling into the mud somewhere behind barbed wire, bleeding to death. Then, I'd have a sort of kiddie orgasm and fall into a contented sleep, to dream about pain, loss and destruction.

You're probably thinking I am trying to blame my violent childhood fantasies on TV, and maybe I am, at that. Remember that show, "My Living Doll"? Julie Newmar played a robot in the shape of a statuesque female, misplaced by the American government and turned up in the bachelor pad of some lucky fool who was too decent a fellow to request her to give him robotic blowjobs. Sexier still, she had a hidden "off" button on the nape of her neck, and when touched there she would go limp and I suppose the bachelor type could have had his merry way with her, though he never did, of course, being such a good American citizen and all. Besides watching the late Elizabeth Montgomery in "Bewitched", who could have satisfied any of her straight husband's fantasies with a twitch of her nose but who instead joyfully cooked him casseroles from scratch, there was Barbara Eden as "Jeannie", who was held in perpetual bondage in a tiny bottle, until she was liberated by her "Master", another good citizen (career military, no less), who steadfastly refused to allow her to satiate him, though she never gave up trying. And let us not forget the character of "Catwoman" in the TV series "Batman" The part was written for Eartha Kitt, who played the feline criminal for a few episodes until either the American public decided she was a little too dark for a starring role or the Johnson administration decided to step up their blacklisting of her for being outspoken against the war in Viet Nam — you choose. I was sorry to see Eartha go, but was promptly rewarded with — yes! — Julie Newmar in Lycra, stilettos, a mask and torpedo tits! My final forays into television bliss were watching Robert Conrad in "Wild, Wild West" do all his own stunts while wearing incredibly tight pants, and, of course, Diana Rigg as "Emma Peel" in "The Avengers." I vowed that someday I'd be just like her — false eyelashes, terrific leather boots, periodically tied up by The Bad Guys.

I was date-raped when I was 17. A friend from another high school arranged a blind date for New Year's Eve, 1975 for me. I went out with the brother of a friend of a friend. His name was Russ and he was several years older than I was. He drove me to a far suburb where about ten people sat around awkwardly and had cocktails. I was quickly tipsy and amorous. He took me into a bedroom and I don't remember what happened next, except I kept saying "No", and I was dropped off at home disheveled, drunk, my clothing torn, to nurse a hangover the next day and feel intense pain in my private parts for about a week. I went back to work at McDonald's and decided right then and there I hated all men. They couldn't be trusted. I became aggressive and flippant with them in my last six months of high school; suddenly, the boys liked me and I was asked out on dates. I led them on and rejected them, usually telling them I suspected I was gay. I enjoyed seeing their confusion.

The year before, I'd had a real sort of boyfriend. His name was Kevin and he was in my creative writing class. I looked like a boy 'til I was nearly twenty. He looked at me one day before class and said, "Lisa, have you ever been to a gay bar?"

"No," I replied, not even knowing what a gay bar was.

"Are you free Friday night?"

"Sure," I said. Oh, boy, a date! I told my parents I was going with some friends to the midnight movies in Cleveland Heights, and Kevin took me to Twiggy's Place in Cleveland. Kevin made it clear he wouldn't touch me, that he was in love with a guy several years older than he who was named Joey, but that he'd enjoy my company at Twiggy's, and I of course agreed, falling instantly in love with Kevin. Twiggy was a transvestite (maybe a transsexual) who ran a little dive down on St. Clair Avenue, near Lake Erie. I was underage, but they let me in. Kevin and I drank Busch beers and he'd split off from me to chat or to cruise with other male patrons. I felt at home in this place, even felt a kind of glamour in it all. Disco music was just becoming big, and it was fun to dance to Gloria Gaynor music. Out in the parking lot, in Kevin's car, we'd smoke pot. I was speechless, crazy in love with him. I understood he wasn't capable of being a real boyfriend to me, but I adored him anyhow.

When I was 18, I tore myself away from the TV set long enough to wander off to a mediocre art school in the Midwest. I needed to figure out some way to earn pocket money to go see Devo when they played in the local beer bar, so I got a job in the art department as a nude model. I also worked as a dishwasher from time to time. Getting naked or scraping garbage off dirty plates and loading a big hot machine really seemed the same to me, as they both paid minimum wage, and they both paid for my growing habit of ordering punk rock records by mail. The nude modeling seemed a little bit easier on the manicure, however, so I guess that is where my preference for posing got solidified.

Around 1976, everyone I knew in art school seemed to be dropping out and moving to New York to be involved in the music scene there, so I did the same a year later. When I told my mother I was going to move to New York and start a new life there, she said to me, "You'll only end up a bum." I was furious with her, cried, and arranged to leave the Midwest promptly and settle in the East Village. Of course, mothers are usually right. I did, indeed, end up a "bum" in many ways.

1. *La Marquise*

The earliest bondage photograph I have of myself was, I think, taken in 1979, in New York City. I was sitting on the floor of the waiting room for a professional dominatrix named La Marquise. I had been working all day as a part-time secretary, five dollars an hour, at a nonprofit fine arts institution uptown, where I worked with their avant-guarde film program.

I was dressed like what I was — a college student. The red sweater probably used to belong to my brother. I found the skirt in a secondhand shop in Ravenna, Ohio. The stockings were textured. This was how I dressed for work in those days. I always wore a chain with a lock around my neck, signifying I was someone's slave. In fact, I wasn't anyone's slave. La Marquise called me "her" slave, but I wasn't "hers" at all. The slave necklace was just for show, when we went out to the clubs.

The white headgear I wore in the photo was leather and was made by a nice amateur in Staten Island. His prices were very reasonable, and he often did barter — he'd give you stuff he'd made in exchange for a session.

La Marquise was about six foot seven in her high heels. She used to be a man, named William Coyote. She had been married, and had been an Army pilot. She was good with computers. She was the first transsexual I'd ever known. I often asked to see her genitals up close (though then La Marquise would often grab the hair of my head and shove my face into her crotch and I was made to lick her artificial cunt), and to touch her silicone breasts. Her pretty blonde hair was curly and fell to her shoulders. She had a deep voice like a man, and had chosen not to have her vocal chords cut to give her a more feminine voice. Penis torture was her specialty. "If I can't do it right, who can?" she'd tell her clients.

She was good at it, and had no fear of surgical needles and piercing. She'd cuddle and comfort her frightened slaves. Then she'd wipe up the blood, turn to me and say, "I'm hungry. Let's go to Little Italy and tie on the feed bag!"

We'd close up shop and she'd switch from one leather catsuit to another. She walked it the way she talked it. Though she liked "straight" female clothes, she usually dressed as a dominatrix all the time. She drove a little TR3. It didn't run very well, but she'd just toss back her head and laugh and throw the car into gear and we'd roar down Fifth Avenue, wire spoke wheels flashing.

In Little Italy, I practiced my Italian on the waiters, and she often made me wear my white leather cuffs, or even metal handcuffs, while I ate. I did so calmly. People did stare, but New York in the late 1970s was full of that kind of thing. No big deal. None of the waiters ever asked, "Why is your date in partial bondage?"

and I do not recall any patrons seated near us asking to be moved because the sight of us offended them.

She taught me to slurp up plates of raw clams — the cherrystones, the big ones — with lots of lemon on them to kill hepatitis. Her wine of choice was Corvo. I could eat two dozen clams in one sitting. She always wanted to sit after each meal, smoke fancy cigarettes, sip fine coffee, and have a Remy Martin. "Let's go," I always said. I wanted to push on, to make another scene.

"You're the `let's go girl'," she'd say. "Do you love me?"

"Don't be stupid," I'd always reply and she'd throw back her curly blonde head and let rip a wave of belly laughs.

She taught me to dress outrageously and to be open about my kinkiness. She'd flirt with both men and women in public. She loved Wo Hop in Chinatown. I preferred Lin's Garden — less good perhaps, but never closed. We ate broiled stray cats and held hands — mine usually cuffed.

I wanted to get to the S/M clubs. We used to go to a small place on 19th Street a lot. A very famous Polish writer was sometimes there, or one of those actresses who hung out with Halston. Being kinky and maybe bi was very trendy in New York in the late '70s. Hard drugs never interested me. I liked to smoke pot. I loved a good meal (I was always hungry) and loved nice wines. Champagne had become my drink of choice. I watched the elegant whores and copied something they did: I learned to order a bottle of champagne, very cold, have it opened, and just drink straight from the bottle (no glass).

I think I was 22. La Marquise ran her dungeon sloppily. She'd pay for her ads in SCREW late. She was often between "phone girls" so I'd answer the phone for her. A lot of the calls were from "phone freaks" But often, a real client appeared for an appointment, and she'd ask him to put his "tribute" in a silver tray with a lid, and then she'd lead him into her large dungeon in the center of her loft in Gramercy Park. I think she charged around $100 for a session. She built all her own suspension equipment and was quite expert at whipping carefully, to cause great pain but leave no lasting marks. She'd lovingly rub oriental analgesic ointment on a wounded slave penis, then watch his face contort as the heat of the ointment kicked in. Though essentially healing in nature, it burned like fire.

La Marquise grew lazy, so hired a "real" phone girl named Cherry and two other dominatrixes, named Annie and Blue. Real outlaw women. They scared me, so I "played nice" with them. One of them, Annie, who hailed from East Lansing, had bad teeth and showed me how she could soak a Desoxyn in distilled water, let it sit a day, then inject the juice with a needle. Directly into her veins. Her skin was a very delicate white and she was a little on the fat side. I waited to see scars and track marks appear on her plump body, but she always seemed to look sleek and well-fed, although her teeth detracted from her looks if she forgot herself and smiled broadly. Otherwise, she looked okay. The reddish hair and David Bowie haircut were a little dated, but overall, I couldn't point at her and say she looked like the played-out intravenous drug user she was.

I knew a lot of hardcore addicts who looked great for many years. Some of them are still alive, and a few of them still look terrific. Go figure.

The phone girl named Cherry needed lots of phone time to talk to her kids in New Jersey. La Marquise never had the heart to charge her for the phone calls. A typical conversation with her kids went like this: "Hi, honey, it's Cherry. Your Mommy. Is Grandma okay? Did you see `Batman' on TV? Yeah? What else did you watch on TV? Did Grandma give you the macaroni and cheese in the box I left in the front room? Did you eat it? Did you play with your video games? Yeah? I love you honey. I'll be home a little late but tomorrow we'll go get cheeseburgers for breakfast, would you like that, honey? Tell your brother not to hit you or I'll crack him one. I love you. Kissies!"

My favorite employee of La Marquise, Blue, was a local gal who lived with a junkie boyfriend whose grandma had willed him a tenement building in the Lower East Side. "My boyfriend's a landlord," she'd say proudly. "And I love how he licks my cunt while I'm vacuuming the place. He just comes right up behind me and sticks his tongue up my minidress. I don't wear no panties."

Blue and her boyfriend, Willie, mostly just collected rents and paid an alcoholic super to do minimal repairs on the slum tenement building they lived in and Willie owned. They not only did heroin, they were also small time dealers. Not very astute ones, from what I gathered. I think Blue arranged a deal that went sour. She disappeared, and I heard she'd been dumped in the East River.

"Some one named Salvatore told me," La Marquise said solemnly. "Don't ask any more questions." I didn't ask any more questions, but I can't forget Blue.

La Marquise began to run with an internationally known biker gang. I don't know what the fuck she was trying to prove. Why would she get involved with those people? One of their members, Crazy Pete, came to visit La Marquise often (he was also friends with Annie). Crazy Pete took one look at me and saw his next victim — or girlfriend — same difference.

I was in bondage and doing a paid session when he first spied me. He just barged into the dungeon and stood there, staring at me. His hair was very long and was bright red. He had a habit of tossing it proudly. I squirmed in my restraints and said, "Hi," as calmly as I could to him. He didn't answer for a long time. I don't know what my paying client thought about all this.

"Are you really a secretary?" Crazy Pete finally asked me, tossing back his red hair.

"Uh, yup," I replied.

"Cool," he said. Then, he walked out. But he came back the next time I worked there. I'd be trying to answer the phones or do sessions, but he'd get in the way, trying to chat me up. He had various proposals. When I indicated I wasn't extremely interested in recreational substance abuse, he started to come up with more "wholesome" ideas.

"You're Pennsylvania Dutch, right?" Yes, I nodded, a gag in my mouth. He'd barged into another paying session. So he came up with "country date" ideas. If he wasn't so scary, this would have been kind of romantic, in a very sick way. First, he wanted to buy me a broken-down racehorse and board it out on the beach in Brooklyn so I could be his little cowgirl. I said no.

Second, he wanted to take me to a country fair out in New Jersey, where there were 4H competitions. Third, he wanted to drive me into the vague countryside in his huge Thunderbird and just drink beer and commune with nature. To his limited credit, he seemed highly impressed with the fact that I really had a secretarial job and needed to keep basic office hours. He promised to untie me from the roof of his car and get me back to the City each morning to work, so I could turn over my small paychecks to him.

His best pal in the gang was called Doubting Thomas. I met Doubting Thomas once, and couldn't get his his face out of my nightmares for the next five or six years. La Marquise should certainly have known better than to mix with the biker crowd. They provided her with a mighty downfall.

While she was sleeping in the back of her loft, the bikers cut the security chain on her elevator, entered, and stole every single item (some of them very costly) from her dungeon. Fortunately, she slept through the whole thing and didn't confront them — I'm sure they would have iced her. She got suddenly smart and wisely hid out in a mental hospital in Manhattan for two weeks after they put the whammy on her, then left town, taking only the little sports car and her beloved rotisserie with her.

She contacted me a few years later, and was on Welfare in Texas and had gained a lot of weight, she said. I cut the phone call short and changed my unlisted number the next day. It had been Annie, the lady from East Lansing, who'd set the whole thing up with her biker pals. She was pissed off because La Marquise had decided at the last minute she didn't want drugs shot up on her premises. Kind of a belated bout of righteousness, if you ask me. I mean, if you've got people shooting up and inviting their biker friends in, don't you think you ought to put a stop to it, oh, say, in the first six months of the activities? Call me square. La Marquise fired Annie, and Annie and her friends took revenge.

The "best" personal slave of La Marquise was named Walter. He had inherited sixty grand from his dead parents, and La Marquise seized it from him to set up her dungeon in Gramercy Park. "I want to marry her," Walter confessed to me, crying, one night. He really loved her.

"Are you sure she's even female?" I asked him. He just cried harder. They lived out in New Jersey most of the time. Walter had a crackerbox house in Edison. He did data entry or programming for a computer company. But he was always late to work, because La Marquise kept him in bondage while she slept in. He kept getting fired. "Tardiness," he'd mutter. She'd beat him up for getting fired each time, even though he'd been fired because she'd left him suspended in the "playroom" and taken a sleeping pill, so of course he couldn't be in Computer Land to punch in on time.

I felt really bad when he'd come home, very frequently, with his final paycheck. La Marquise told him to shut up and run out for groceries. She seemed to always want to celebrate. She was a good cook. She made a lovely pepper steak, and she and I would sit at the kitchen table in the crackerbox house and chow down, and poor Walter had his hands cuffed behind his back, and a choker collar around his neck. He had his own dog bowl to eat from, off the floor. His wine was dumped right on top of the meal, for him to slurp up. I don't see how he managed to eat his pepper steak all bent over and collared like that, but he usually did okay.

Instead of soy sauce, his meals tended to be salted with his own tears. I felt rotten about it all but kept quiet. I wish I could find Walter now and tell him I'm sorry, but that would be pretty lame, wouldn't it?

Staying with La Marquise was always a gamble. She was never on time. Always late. Whether it was driving poor Walter to work or getting me to my secretarial job in Manhattan on weekdays, or even keeping a high-paying session in her dusty dungeon in Gramercy Park. She'd wake up late, groan, take a very long shower using only excellent toiletries, and then grind up fresh coffee beans, and force me to sit down and eat Italian pastries we'd bought in Little Italy the night before.

I'd go take a shower myself, picking up her wet towel from the floor to reuse. She seldom had fresh ones available unless Walter had taken out the wash to the laundromat, something he was often reluctant to do, as she generally made him wear handcuffs out in public (and kept losing the keys). I'd try to get clean and wash the smell of her artificial cunt off my face.

She'd tear open the shower curtain and monitor my use of her beauty products. "Don't use so much of my Vidal Sassoon creme rinse," she'd chide me. A full hour after I was supposed to be at work, we'd get into her little sports car and tool into Manhattan, laughing and flashing our tits to fellow travelers of the road, on the way.

By this point, my mood was generally improved. The weeping Walter had been dropped off at his computer job, and I was full of fresh coffee, Italian pastries, and a shot or two of fine cognac. La Marquise liked to crash into other cars in the tunnel on the way into Manhattan. When they'd go too slow for her, she'd either rearend them, or else sideswipe them. I've known a lot of New York drivers like this. I don't know what gets into them.

My boss was understanding when I'd finally show up to type and answer the phones. There I was, in semen-stained tight black leather, and he pretended to believe my story that we'd been in a car accident in the Holland Tunnel. Nice boss. In fact, my story was partially true. We'd been in a crash, but we had been the ones who'd caused it, and we'd peeled rubber and skidded away, guilty.

"Just get to work, Lisa," he'd say. He never specified that I be on time, so I kept the job nearly two years. After work, there I was, always back at the dusty dungeon in Gramercy Park, answering her phones and trying to book her a last appointment so we could go out to eat in style before everything shut down in Manhattan around five a.m.

She taught me to love Sweet's Restaurant, oldest in New York, in what was at the time an abandoned South Street Seaport. She taught me to have cocktails only at Windows on the World, as the food there was lousy and it was more fun just to have the view while you were getting drunk, she explained. She was right about many things. The food at Sweet's was costly but delicious, and a fifty dollar tip got you a table on the "right" side of Windows on the World. There was a sushi chef to make you little munchies while you sipped champagne and got tired of the view in six or seven minutes.

Then, it was on to a steak house for the beginning of the evening. Dinner was also often at an Italian place near Hester and Mott, and afterward, her favorite place for dessert was an Italian coffee bar just around the corner. She always needed a liqueur after each orgy of food. She is to blame for my bad personal habits now. She drank all day and all night. So did I. I could retire now on all the money I've thrown away on drink over these many years.

We stayed in touch for years, but when she finally moved back to her ancestral home in Newport about a decade later, I avoided her. She sensed the snub, and never called me again. Where is she today? Did she die of those silicone tits? Did she trust one client too many? And why did I trust her?

One night, at her slave Walter's place out in New Jersey, we had showered and gone to bed and were having sex. I scrutinized her massive cunt, as usual. "Take it," she moaned. I did. I started to lick and slurp it, and it seemed to take five minutes to get from the top to the bottom, it was so big. Also, it didn't taste or seem like a real woman's cunt. That is the truth. But I licked it as much as I could and nibbled on her nipples and next morning, she declared, "I'm in love." Uhoh, I thought.

One night, I met her after my secretarial job, and she plopped handcuffs on me and led me to her little sports car. "Weekend in the country!" she cried, cheerily. As we plunged through the Lincoln Tunnel, I prayed a little. I'm not religious. But it seemed a good idea to pray at that moment in time.

We drove to Sea Bright. A man known as The Corporal had rented a farmhouse and filled it with working kinky whores. He had party weekends, and for about $20 a head, you got let in and got soft drinks, cold cuts, and the run of the place. We brought our own bottle — everyone else had, too. I was wearing a white blouse and peasant dress, with lacing up the bodice. As the guests appraised me, one chanted, "She has such submissive eyes."

I prayed La Marquise would protect me from this pack of wolves. To her credit, she did, for the most part. "No one plays with my slave unless I say so," she announced. I felt better. I had a vodka and Coke and a ham sandwich. The ham was two or three days old and very dry. I chased it with a couple of limp pickles and some heavily sugared cole slaw. We went around the farmhouse and met the other players for the weekend. One, named Anastasia, was in full corset and eyed me hungrily. I feared her mightily. To say she eyed me hungrily surely sounds clichéd... but trust me on this one.

I was quickly stripped, cuffed and taken to the play room, where the evening's ceremonies were about to be announced. It must have been a den or study, back when the farmhouse was used for "normal" stuff. The host read us an extremely long list of some rules for the sex play, such as, "Stop when the skin breaks." After he was done reading all the rules, he announced, "Let the games begin!"

First order of the evening was a wife who needed to be punished. "She has a fantasy of all the men here whipping her for her naughty fantasy," the husband announced. The men lined up, cheerfully. The wife, about 40 and with a chunky bod, removed her flimsy night dress and, nude, bent over a vaulting "horse" Each man delivered a few blows, but after about the 20th man, she was about to bleed. She was inspected by the "house doctor", and it was declared, regrettably, the game must stop. To her credit, she made not a sound during the whippings and paddlings, which were severe and done with full force.

We then saw a man who had done his wife up as a genuine ponygirl. He explained she was a little too frail for him to actually mount, but there was a special saddle for her back, anyway, just for show. She had full headgear and lovely green feathers in her headdress. A strict bit (the curb type) was in her mouth. La Marquise stripped me naked, then hogtied me in front of a fireplace. She wandered away and forgot me. I started to sob, which is dangerous when you are gagged (you can choke to death).

I heard a man lie quietly behind me, masturbating. As my sobs intensified, so did his level of stimulation. "Ah, yes," he sighed. "There is nothing more erotic than the sound of a woman's tears."

We were not to sleep there that night, though that would have been possible, had we brought sleeping bags. La Marquise took me to a room full of corseted dominas. "Can we play with your slave?" Anastasia asked. I felt true fear.

"Maybe later," La Marquise said. Gratefully, I was lead away, and permitted to have another helping of tepid cole slaw.

We drove back to Manhattan just before dawn. The cute little sports car purred. La Marquise was chuckling. "We have to go out for dessert," she declared.

"It's five in the morning!" I protested.

"Just perfect for coffee in Little Italy," she murmured. She boldly pounded on a closed door, and we were let in and served espresso and pastries, which I was too tired to consume, but poked at anyway, as much out of fear as of politeness.

I was subsequently dropped off at the door to my job. I had the front door key, let myself into the mansion on 69th Street, and found a couch to nap on for a couple of hours. Until I was discovered by Raoul the cleaning man, bruised and muttering in my sleep. He looked at me wide-eyed. Surely, I smelled awful. And was full of whip marks.

"Are you okay?" he asked me.

"Sure," I answered, "I was just out partying. Don't say nothing to the boss please. I'm gonna go wash up in the toilet now. Can you make sure there's some coffee brewing in the lunch room?" He nodded and split. I went to the toilet, ran a lot of hot water in the sink, stripped, and washed myself from head to toe with industrial soap, even my hair, which I dried with paper towels.

I went and got some coffee and put back on my raincoat over my clothes. No one asked why I wore it that day at work — it sure did cover a multitude of sins. The phones began ringing at nine, the boss got in about half an hour later. By then, I was fairly perky, and was diligently typing royalty statements for our stable of artists. I quit work around three to attend my Hunter College class in Buddhism.

Back in the late seventies, pot smoking was permitted in the Hunter hallways. I inhaled a joint and went into my lecture, which focused on the concept of Hungry Ghosts. A Hungry Ghost is a very bad reincarnation. You come to Earth with a huge belly and a tiny mouth and a throat so narrow, you can only swallow one grain of cooked rice at a time. You are damned to live out your life in a state of perpetual dissatisfaction.

2. *Lili*

I have a photo of us together. We are fully clothed, handcuffed together, smoking and chuckling. What a dear gal Lili was. I pray she still lives and is well. I know her real name, but since she is not American, I do not know how to track her.

Her real name is Sueda. She is from a Far Eastern country, and has a husband in Norway. I did not understand why they were separated, but she made such a sad face when I asked about her marital status, I did not press her further. I bore a resemblance to Jodie Foster at the time. I was constantly mistaken for her. Taxi drivers would pick me up in the East Village, and would say, "It's you. I can't fucking believe it."

There I was, at 13th and 3rd, frantically waving down a Checker cab (those were always my favorite — you liked them, too, right?). My horn-rimmed glasses and business suits only convinced the deranged cabbies all the more it was really "me" — their very own "Jodie."

In 1981, right after I had a perm, was thin, and had an Italian suntan, I was mistaken for Linda Blair. Conversation One: "It's you!"

"What?"

"Jodie! You're Jodie Foster!"

"No, thank you, that's very flattering. I'm not. 23rd and 7th, please."

"I dig it, you're afraid of stalkers. You know, I am just like that crazy taxi driver. I guess I shouldn't be telling you this."

"Mind if I smoke pot in your cab?"

"No, it will be an honor! Hey, can I have your autograph?" (I roll a joint. I am neat, efficient, and it is lit in a minute. I puff.)

"Doll baby, I'll give you my autograph." (I do.)

"But it don't say `Jodie'."

"But I'll tell ya the truth — I am a porn actress, call girl, and bondage model. Save that. It will be worth money some day!"

"Wow, you are already a celeb!"

"I kind of am, just a sleazy one. Do you really think I look like Jodie?"

"I still think you're her. You're faking so I don't abduct you!"

"Well, my main objection to being abducted, if you think I'm Jodie, is that not only will my boyfriend worry and my boss miss his secretary, but you will eventually figure out I'm not `me' and you might get mad and off `me.'"

"I could," the cabbie admitted.

"And we wouldn't want that, would we?" I continued. Fortunately, our ride was nearing its end.

"Well, I would kinda like it," the cabbie confessed. I laughed hard and rolled another joint.

"Hey, you want me to roll you a bomber? Like for a tip?"

"Nah, I don't smoke," he said, as we passed the Bellmore Cafeteria. "But my friend likes a smoke. So give me one for him — I can swap him for somethin', later."

"Okay." I roll. He looks at me in his rearview mirror. He has the De Niro face, even a Mohawk and the military jacket. As I pay him, tip him well, and run for my destination, he shouts, "G'night, Jodie. You're a sweet lady. I'm gonna tell 'em all you're a real doll. I know you can't let on it's really you. That's cool." I stop, dead in my tracks, and turn. He is sneering, and lighting up a cigarette. He nods to some imaginary music in his skull. There is nothing I can say to change his mind.

"Well, you know how it is," I say, wave, and he nods in satisfaction. He drives off. My Taxi Driver. Oh, my Travis.

Conversation Two: "You're that actress, right?" East Village, early 1980s.

"Which one?"

"The Exorcist girl."

"No! Oh, shit, that is funny! Do I really look like her?" (He is very serious, this cabbie.)

"Well — yeah. I know it's you."

"Oh, hey, that is a great compliment. I adore her. Wasn't the sequel cool? But my name is Lisa. I'm just an East Village punk and I need to get to work. I'm only a receptionist. Really!" He looks down, grabs a smoke, lights up, and continues to drive, while peering at me in his rearview mirror.

"I know, I know, you gotta say that. Where's your bodyguard?"

"Do you think I need one? Are you gonna abduct me?"

"No, honey, but think about it." (I do. Not funny.)

"Well, let's just say I am Linda Blair. Who I am not. What would you like to say to `me'?"

"You are a good actress and the bad reviews... fuck 'em! We all love ya, your public." I pause.

"Really? You think I am a good actress?"

"Yeah. Real good. And now that I see ya close up, shit, you're so pretty. You don't need all that makeup they throw on you. Naw. You's too pretty just natural. You fight 'em, girl."

"Well, I am not Linda Blair, but thank you, anyway."

"Is you an actress?"

"Well, yeah, but just porno and bondage stuff."

"Okay, cool. I knew you was an actress, by your face. I was right, huh?"

"Yeah, man, you was right, but you got the wrong actress here — if I am an actress."

"Okay, sweetie," he says. We have arrived at my job. He gets out to open the cab door for me — very rare in New York. "You'se a good actress. And you'se gonna have a good future. I am a judge of these things."

"I will never forget you," I promise him, then go to work.

Lili had worked as a topless dancer in New York before I met her. I had heard the bosses at the stripper agency she worked at were very hard cases. She claimed she showed up for her last week's pay and they pretended not to know her. Money down the drain! But what could Lili do? She showed me a little g-string with beads she wore on her tiny hips. The g-string was white satin and the beads were in gold. That was all she wore. Since she didn't have the spare money to buy a new S/M outfit, she was displayed on the floor with the rest of us whores in her little g-string, with a skimpy top hiding her small breasts. We were mostly in leather, Lili was still in her size five high-heeled pumps and that minuscule beaded g-string. Our house regulars always wanted to try "the new girl", so she was quickly working, doing both dominant and submissive sessions.

Until she gained her confidence, she did more sub than dom stuff. "What will I do weeeeth them, Eleeeeezabeth?" she asked me.

"You mean, slaves?" I replied, bingeing on ice cream and not looking up. "Shit, you got high heels on. Just put them down on the floor and walk all over them. Keep doing it for 60 minutes. Call them names. At the last ten minutes, flip them over and take off your shoes and crush their dicks with your bare feet. If your feet are dirty, make them lick and suck your toes. They'll squirt. Just remember, don't fuck them. This isn't a sex place. And we don't hustle for tips."

"Okay, I see that. Thanks," she said.

A week or so later, I heard her tiny voice, shouting, "Suck my toes, you dirty, dirty peeeeeeeg!" I heard a grunt, and then five minutes later, the client left in a hurry, sixty dollars poorer but carrying a lighter load of sperm in his sleazy balls. "You're learning fast, honey," I told her and gave her a pat and a squeeze.

"Theeeees not so bad," she said. "Eeet better than those top-less agencies who keep my last week's pay."

"That's the spirit!" I replied, and hugged her.

She felt so tiny in my arms. Somehow, in that dirty place, she had managed to keep herself clean and smelling all right. (Our shower had gone out of order the year before.) I gave her my real name and phone number, and invited her over to meet The Professor. The Professor took a picture of us, relaxing before one of our joint bondage modeling sessions for him. "Don't worry," I told her. "This guy is really, really cool. He doesn't want to fuck us. He might jerk off, but we don't even have to look. He's fast. He likes his models without makeup, and light bondage, in disciplinary scenarios. There's no real pain involved, unless I ask for it in advance Then, I make extra money, cuz he tapes my screams — so I charge him a little more for this. He's retired and on a fixed income, so he can't pay top dollar, but his checks never bounce and he'll buy us a modest restaurant meal afterward, if we're hungry. He's a solid repeat customer. I've been seeing him about once a month for years now. I've never raised my price with him. I've even slept at his house and met one of his sons."

Lili was impressed. His Hollywood career, wartime adventures, and life in Academe also added to his cachet. I posed with Lili for him sometimes in Brooklyn, in a friend's apartment, and once, we went up to The Professor's house in Chappaqua. I retired from the life of a dominatix/submissive after two full years in The Grand Central of Sleaze, on 23rd Street (described in a later chapter of this book). I worked there from 1982/84, then gathered my earnings and used them to pay tuition to go to graduate school, to get an M.B.A. I stayed in touch with some clients and working girls, and Lili was one I stayed in touch with for quite a few years, until I finally lost track of her.

She was a seamstress, it seemed, and aspired for "real" work in the garment industry. I introduced her to some friends who owned a trendy fashion boutique in the East Village, and she ended up staying and being their shopgirl for a year, earning a few extra dollars by running a sewing machine in the back space to make punk outfits for a new type of client, called a "yuppie."

I never had sex with Lili, but used to touch her often, fondly. She was too sweet to hit on. Also, it was clear she was in love with that faraway husband in Norway. Last I heard from her, she was out of The Life entirely, living up in Westchester, and had a job in a couture house. In the mid1980s, I considered, very briefly, opening up my own House of Ill Repute, and I invited her to a little casual party at my apartment in Brooklyn, to discuss employment with me. She was reserved. I think she had seen her way out of The Life, and wasn't that anxious to return. More power to her. So I never became her madam. We just stayed friends.

Often, when it was a quiet night on 23rd Street and I was busy with my regular clients and she had nothing to do, I'd get the client to pay a little more to have her come into our cubicle and observe my session. I like to think I taught her a lot. When I am submissive, I submit gently and quietly, reminding the tricks that

I bruise easily. When I am dominant, I ask if marks are a problem — i.e., is there a wife or girlfriend at home who will notice a whipsting? I used to kiss and hug slaves often, tell them they were good little boys at the end of the session. Sometimes they'd cry and cling to me and say, "Thank you, Mistress. You are so kind."

After my worst spankings, I'd croon to them and caress them and put ointment on their red behinds. "Mistress is so sorry she had to be harsh with you, but Timmy, you know you've been so bad!"

"Yes, Mistress. I have been."

"So, now you're punished. Go forth and sin no more — this week. When you sin next week, come back, and I will give you that spanking you need."

"Thank you, Mistress," he'd snuffle, then shuffle off to Buffalo.

"Hey, Slave?" (They often gave their names as John, or Tom.) "Next time you come, could you bring me a nice cold beer? Michelob. This way, I get a drink, and I can golden shower train you if you're ready for that."

"Oh, yes, Mistress. Just one bottle?"

"Yeah, I can't get in trouble with the management here for one beer, if I tell them it's so I can piss on you afterward."

"Okay, Mistress."

"You take care, now. Be a good boy. Save your sixty dollars and come back to see me. I don't need any tips, just be a regular slave. That means more to me."

"I know, Mistress. You are one of the good ones."

"Your time is up now, slave. See ya next week, I hope?"

"Next week I have a wedding to attend, but I may come by soon after that. Just before closing."

"Okay, but call first, and don't drive if you're too drunk. Bring me a piece of cake! Or at least some sugared almonds!"

"I will Mistress. I love you."

"I love you too, slave."

3. *The Professor*

I was introduced to The Professor, who worked as a dean at a very prestigious New York City University, by a writer/ junkie/film buff/Wall Street systems analyst I knew who kept hounding me to introduce him to filmmaker Kenneth Anger. I worked with Kenneth Anger at my job in the fine arts institution, so had his home address. (I typed up his royalty statements and mailed him his royalty checks.) I refused to arrange a personal introduction, but offered to forward a letter to Mr. Anger. Mr. Anger responded to the letter, and they eventually met. In gratitude for my forwarding the letter and facilitating the meeting, I was introduced to The Professor. They had met at Movie Star News, which was still on 14th Street in those days. They were both rifling through, of course, the bondage photos.

The writer said something like, "Do you want to meet a real bondage model — for hire?" The Professor, whose name is Fred, said yes, of course. A meeting was arranged at the Hunan Taste restaurant on Second Avenue near St. Marks. (My friends referred to it as "The Human Waste" It was a ptomaine palace.) The moment we met, Fred recognized me, the girl in all the peep shows

up on 42nd Street, back in 1980. He smiled and nodded. Hungry
shark. Me — shark bait.

We ate a simple Chinese meal, and it was arranged that the
writer would escort me to Fred's house in Chappaqua on the Metro
North train. The writer was to receive roundtrip train tickets and
about $40 finder's fee. I was to receive roundtrip fare, plus $75. I
was very young. Maybe 23. My first marriage, to Wolfe, was
already going sour. I was beginning to figure out he was a junkie.

Fred put a chain and leash around me, I was lightly bound,
and the writer led me around for some photos. The Gibson Girl
hairstyle was my "thing" at the time — I went often to an old
Polish beautician in my East Village neighborhood for lacquered
bouffant hairdos. As they slowly got messed up over the course of
the following week, I'd sweep up the huge mass of ratted hair and
give myself a sort of punk Gibson Girl coif. I thought it looked
really cool with my black leather motorcycle jacket.

The writer soon tired of the relationship, the threesome.
"I'm not a pimp," he declared, which struck me as very weird,
since it was he who had introduced me to a male client and took a
small fee each time. The male client had a sexual urge — that was
the only reason, initially, for the meetings. Isn't that pimping? I
think so. We went down to the basement of Fred's suburban house.
Most of the curtains had been carefully closed. In future years,
Fred was less clandestine, and I enjoyed sitting on his back porch,
wearing one of his wife's robes, and watching the spiders spin their
webs in the dewy evenings while I sipped pear brandy. "You'll get

sick," Fred cautioned. My feet were bare. I'd smoke pot out on the porch, which didn't bother him as much as my bare feet propped up in the cool air.

"I'm already sick," I'd reply. He'd just shake his head and go back in the house.

Of course, I fell in love with Fred, though it was a bizarre type of love, since we'd never made out or had normal intercourse. And he's 39 years my senior. Our birthdays are close to each other — we're both Gemini. I stayed over at his house for many weekends, modeling a little and doing some secretarial work, never raising my price. Someone very famous in Hollywood, where Fred had worked after the Second World War, had taught him how to make perfect scrambled eggs, so I was always hungry for breakfast at The Professor's creepy old house. We also carefully reserved a glass of champagne for my breakfast — maybe even half an eclair.

He'd drive me to the train station in Chappaqua, and I'd catch the express train to my jobs in Midtown, already missing Fred, wishing those 39 years of age difference between us weren't there at all. Fred turned out to be perhaps my steadiest client, for 20 years at least. He is about 82, and I fear I will lose him soon — he has cancer. Every time he calls me in Europe, and I hear his voice, I thank God he is still independent. I saw him in person recently and he looked great and seemed extremely fit. He didn't seem to be 82 years old at all — he seemed quite a bit younger. I would never have guessed a malignancy was then growing in his abdomen.

He is in his third marriage. His children are grown, and his third wife lives in Switzerland, where she writes technical tracts for a large pharmaceutical concern. They communicate by fax. Apparently, she is jealous of me. Jealous of what, exactly, I wonder? I wonder how much she knows? He never put his penis in me. He never put his tongue in my mouth. I cannot even recall his grabbing my small breasts. He has warmed my butt with belts, switches, and his hand. He's put clothespins on my tongue when I talked too much.

We had such fun, cooking dinners together. Almost always we had bargain basement Spanish sparkling wine, frozen eclairs, London Broil, and salads, which he shuddered as he watched me mix, as I never measure the vinaigrette ingredients, but the salad dressing usually comes out just fine anyway. (I stress the "usually.") A fire in the fireplace. Sometimes we'd watch an S/M movie together. How cozy! We certainly didn't date in the "normal" sense. Our goodbye dinner, just before his third marriage in 1985, was at Bill's Gay Nineties on 54th Street in Manhattan. The second floor dining room. Fred ordered orange duck, but I was too upset for anything but martinis. I began to cry. I knew I was losing him to his new wife. It was pouring rain outside, and though he sheltered me with his umbrella, by the time we got to the F train, I was half-soaked. "I don't care," I muttered, turning my back on him, and went home, very damp in polyester, to my second husband, hating the world.

But I did care. My heart was breaking. Years later, the writer called me and begged me to help him find a job. "Why can't you get a job yourself?" I asked. "You're got an M.B.A. and are a systems analyst with Wall Street experience."

"I've gotten into junk," he told me flatly. Oh, no, I thought — I can't handle this, not after my first marriage was ruined by that drug.

"Have you cleaned up?" I asked.

"Pretty much," he said, but sounded alarmingly uncertain. "I smoke good quality pot now to get high," he continued. I felt slightly reassured, until I saw him in the flesh. I was terribly shocked by his appearance. He was thin as a squirrel, and always wore long sleeves to hide his needle marks. He chainsmoked and had dark brown teeth stained heavily by tobacco.

I got him a job as a word processor in the junk bond department of the brokerage firm that employed me at the time. We'd take lunch breaks together and he'd walk me through Central Park and give me pot to smoke. He was doing his level best to stay away from hard drugs. He'd found a girlfriend. I hear they are married now and have a kid.

Six months after I got him the job in my department at the brokerage firm, he turned on me. The latenight phone calls began, strange voices moaning, "Yer a cunt." I guess you just can't trust a junkie. The nasty phone calls continued, so often that my answering machine broke. Before things went wrong, I had been visiting the writer's East Village apartment, and I looked up at his ceiling and saw blood up there. "How'd that get there?" I asked.

"How d'ya think?" was his only reply. Junkies. I've never been to Planet Junkie, myself. Never want to make that trip. I've seen too many people reduced to trash by heroin, so I've never tried it.

Fred didn't like to see me in heavy makeup. Further, I was not to fuss with garter belts and stockings. He preferred me nude. He liked simple bondage, such as handcuffs, thumb cuffs, and leather straps. He liked basement dungeon settings, and real jail cells when he could find them. (He had an old iguana cage which looked pretty scary.) I was always alone in the pictures, for the most part kneeling on a cold, hard floor, looking very sad. The forgotten penitent. In fact, I never knelt for more than five or ten minutes, my poses were just until he could get the shot, and there was always hot tea and a sip of champagne waiting for me just beyond camera range. Then, a hot bath, a hair washing, and a fire in the fireplace at night I played with his aging dog, "Snoopy", and his Burmese Python, "Snaps." I'd watch TV and pilfer his vodka. We'd go shopping together at the big grocery store in his town. "The Port Salut looks good," he'd mutter.

"What's that?" I'd say.

"It's a type of European cheese, my dear," he'd chuckle, shaking his head at my ignorance.

The Professor started introducing me to his other amateur kinky photographer friends. To a one, they were all very nice people. One was known only as "Phil", and had been a ballet dancer. In his dotage, he ran a dance costume company. His mother was still alive, but legally blind. He put her to work each day, sewing sequins on cute little pairs of tap pants, or simple piece work of some sort. "Keeps her active," he declared.

Phil would breeze into town, we'd spend a few hours taking pictures, and then he'd take us out to a marvelous dinner. Once, we ate Swiss food in a chalet-type place. Rack of lamb, potato pancakes, etc. Good wine. We tumbled home, thanked him, and he gave me $200. Later, he sent me character shoes, since I was taking dance classes to learn the Lindy at the time, and he also sent me fishnet stockings I wore to my part-time work as a whore. The professor spent hours alone, cutting up magazines and making collages, all by hand. He liked a woman's hands in handcuffs. Her head bowed. Hair messy. Shifting weight from one leg to another, to give her tired feet a break while she waited for her jailer to come and mete out her just deserts.

In my case, the desserts were usually eclairs. The Professor was born and raised in Germany — in a large city. He came from a good family. But to the Nazis, he was Jew because he had a Jewish parent. He asked for permission to visit the 1939 World's Fair in New York, was granted that permission, and he never looked back. He went to Oberlin College in Ohio, then drifted to Hollywood, where he was the personal secretary for a movie star and ran with the "kraut crowd" He married and divorced a starlet. During the War, he enlisted on the American side, in psychological warfare. He moved back East after the War, married a sweetheart, and had children. He got a good job with a radio station in New York. "I've found the American dream," he felt sure. But the wife was mentally ill and alcoholic. She hid gin in Tupperware and started writing to a black lifer. The lifer got out, moved in, and attempted to take The Professor's wife with him off to a good life in Chicago, on the streets, selling encyclopedias. The wife died a few weeks later.

4. *Ania*

New York may be the world's largest small town. A year or so after I'd become friendly with Ania I mentioned her to my friend Rowan. "Oh, I know her," Rowan said immediately. "We went to the same high school."

"I think she's a junkie," I continued, a propos to nothing.

"Always has been," Rowan replied. Not an unusual little conversation for a warm Spring afternoon on Park Avenue, but I couldn't help but be amazed. "There are eight million stories in the Naked City..." and Rowan, my co-worker in a semi-reputable investment banking house where we both worked, happened to know the same young woman I did — Ania. ("Only in New York.")

I held my breath as we walked, for two reasons. One, we were smoking a joint. Rowan's brother Patrick was a part-time drug dealer, and she almost always had a joint for our lunch breaks. Two, I was afraid Rowan would ask how I knew Ania. I hadn't yet revealed to Rowan that I was a part-time prostitute specializing in the kinky stuff. Rowan, however, didn't ask. Either she was too stoned to care by this point, or she figured I knew Ania from the East Village, my hangout.

Rowan's favorite topic is her personal life, so the subject soon switched to her current boyfriend. One of the reasons I liked Rowan was that she was like a TV set always tuned to a soap opera — a TV you kept running on low volume, to keep yourself company — to distract yourself from yourself. Most of my friends found her horrifically superficial, but I value superficiality greatly. Superficial people make great colleagues, friends — even lovers — in my book. They spout platitudes and accept platitudes in return. Nothing heavy, thank you. No philosophy today, thank you. Keep the conversation light; or better still, LITE. America! God knows, living and working in New York City is sensory overload enough. If you can make it there you'll make it anywhere, but chances are, also, that you're mentally ill, or at the very least, maladjusted.

Each day can be quite literally a very struggle for life itself, so you often find New Yorkers with lots of "lite" social contacts, like my bubbled-headed Rowan, who'd toss away $200 on a haircut and dye job, spend a few nights drinking midtown, and then cry to me that she was broke. And two days later, she'd be wearing a smashing new designer suit her mother had found for some incredible price, and given to her out of twisted, angstladen, Irish-Catholic guilt I never understood and certainly didn't want to know about. Which was a good reason, Rowan rationalized, to go shopping for new shoes: because her mother had spent so little, given it for nothing, and didn't it make Rowan look slimmer? Of course it did, and sure, Rowan deserved those new shoes. That's what credit cards are for, right?

Understanding Rowan helped me to understand Ania a little because both are from the same area in Queens — Middle
Village. Ania's from Ridgewood actually, but Middle Village is the
next neighborhood adjacent, and both are in the middle of
nowhere. Queens, New York, is something that has to be seen to
be believed, and if you believed your eyes, you probably still could
not grasp the spirit of this suburban, sprawling piece of hell.
Queens is horrible, when you consider it as a whole, but when
you're in places like Rowan's mother's house there, you begin to
find yourself profoundly in doubt of your own value judgments. In
many ways, Queens is as bland and pedestrian as any boring, bleak
section of any blue collar, middle-class enclave you'll find anywhere in the U.S.A., but there's a sort of tension in Queens that's
completely unique.

Look to the West and you'll see, on a clear day, the famous
New York City skyline. Look to the East and there lies Long Island,
over a hundred miles long, tract houses, mansions, beaches, toxic
waste sites... look up, and you'll see, very often, the bluest sky ever,
making you even more aware of the grayness around you. Look
down, and it isn't hard to imagine that just below the pavement lies
hell. Queens can be such a super mind fuck. I mean, all around you
are concrete (literally) reminders of middle class aspirations — private homes, little gardens, cars in driveways, and Barbeque pits. You
find yourself enjoying these shallow things, and perhaps, even cov-
eting them. And yet, just on the horizon is the grotesque reminder
of how difficult it is to earn these bourgeois trappings.

The skyscrapers are like teeth, tearing at the unhealthy (yet often so blue!) atmosphere, and you find yourself thinking, "It is truly a jungle out there." And the anxieties mount, and you worry about next month's bills, so you can have a drink or something else to relax a little, and ultimately, you go too far, thus blowing your budget, thus making yourself more worried about money, and so on.

It's mental traps and money traps like this that lead people to lives of part-time prostitution. The extra money is needed to pay for your bad judgements, and the work is part-time because you want to keep one foot as solidly as possible in Real Life. But you don't like Real Life — especially when Real Life is Life in Queens.

I met Ania in January 1982, I think. That's the month I started working in the Grand Central of Sleaze — Jack's Cheap S/M whorehouse on 23rd Street. I started working there because I'd managed to stop working as a call girl the year before, having found work as a receptionist in a Madison Avenue public relations firms, but I'd fallen in love with a writer and he wanted me to get my own apartment and cook him nice dinners, so I needed more money. He often showed up late for dinner, and always promised to share the rent, but didn't for nearly two years. I ended up marrying the guy. Yes, I'm an asshole. But I'm a resourceful asshole, thank you.

The city never sleeps and neither does my neurotic Pennsylvania Dutch brain. When all else fails — sell yourself. And if your looks aren't quite good enough to work for a Mayflower madam, and you happen to own a lot of black leather attire and a pair of shoes with 6-inch spike heels, you go into kinky prostitution. Doesn't much matter, the year. S/M is kind of timeless. Certainly the older a woman gets, the more she can charge. This is one profession where you can certainly demand more money based on your level of expertise.

The greatest mistakes are made by people whose hearts are too soft, too good. There's a true sort of Darwinism to all this: only the tough survive. The soft are consumed by their own slaves, or worse, by their own slavery to their own weaknesses.

Ania isn't really tall, but she seems somehow a little larger-than-life. "Statuesque" might be a good description of this Nordic Ice Goddess from deepest Ridgewood. Ania has been to me like one of those puzzles with 5,000 tiny interlocking pieces. There it sits, on your card table. You find yourself horrified that you're actually sitting there, trying to assemble it. Years go by, and you blow off the dust and the pieces fit, slowly, and the total picture emerges. And what, you wonder, will you do with it when it's finished? The image you're struggling to put together (you realize from the outset) is tacky. It's banal. Yeah, it's in the worst taste. Yet you find it compelling. You somehow believe, almost, that once you've mastered the joining of those maddening little pieces, you're going to possess something more. You'll have some sense of achievement. Because there's a kind of... beauty to it all. A horrid, superficial beauty — a high gloss over sleazy cardboard. It may be horrid, but dammit, it's gonna take effort, and once you've done it, it's yours.

Ania seemed like such a thing, when I first saw her answering the phones for Jack, arranging 'appointments' for Jack's sleazy whores. Ania seemed easy to judge, but fifteen years later I still find myself looking for her. You could certainly call her one of my obsessions. To rank her among my bad habits would be to diminish her, however, and this I won't stand for. I worship Ania.

Because I'm a former 'Mistress' (dominatrix), I'm used to pointing a finger and having my slaves admire the crazy things I do. Who cares about their opinions, huh? They're paying me. Turn, then, your thoughts to Manhattan. In 1982. In Gramercy Park. On the second floor of a crummy two-story building, in a neighborhood which houses an art school of extremely questionable standing and two or three dozen brothels, where you can choose from a thoroughly depressing selection of messed up females, there for you to deal with in cubicles with dusty wall-to-wall carpeting, cheap plywood walls and damp platform beds with dirty linen so threadbare you could make out the bloodstains on the foam padding beneath it. $60 for an hour with a woman who will "dominate" you. No tipping required, and very little forthcoming. Look behind the pressboard furniture and discover a treasure trove of rusty needles hidden by junkies long gone, or long dead, and always long forgotten. What counts is only today, and your craving for pizza, and that stack of bills somewhere in your kitchen. What counts is Ania, with her sweet blue eyes, passing you a joint of exotic smoke, Ania who's got three guys booked for you at ten, and she thinks one of them's "for real."

A good phone girl earns every penny of her 10% of the

gross. She tirelessly delivers her spiel to the phone freaks, the curious, the tourists and the few cheap, demented hard cases who actually frequent the premises; these weirdos often deriving obvious pleasure from seeing the "Mistress" and the "slave girls" paraded before them in the corridor, having probably sampled the wares of each previously and knowing each sleazy life story, and just how much, and why, those dollars are needed. Each woman will keep only $30 from each dominant session, and after she's paid $10 to the "Hawkeye" (sort of mini-pimp, employed by the management), and paid for her new stockings, and her cab rides to and from work, and the vices of her lover, and the substances she has to abuse to deal with showing up at work, there's not much left. In short, a job, like most others, but this one being tax-free.

And there I'd dwell, two or three times a week, often after work at my "straight" jobs, and all day and all night on Sunday. 12 to 15 hours a week on the New York City subway. 40 hours a week in Wall Street, kissing white male ass for horrid wages, and then, kissing or whipping the same horrid white ass, only this time, becoming intimately aware of the pimples thereon, the smelly feet, and the statements: "Don't leave any marks." Yes, they have wives. Yes, they are paying you. And yeah, they may be on their knees, but guess who works for whom and what will happen if the customer ain't satisfied?

Ania sat in the filthy chair, and she booked our tricks. I stared at her body. It was nice, but she was no conventional beauty, and she knew she didn't have the "software" to be "on the floor" with us... or did she? We spent idle hours bingeing on pot and ice cream, laughing about our naive forays into Europe, where we thought we may have tasted "culture" but we couldn't really be sure. All we knew was that our meaty butts had suddenly been beautiful to the men of those foreign lands, and we'd realized, for sure, that money equals freedom, and freedom equals an increase of choices, and this equals a greater opportunity to escape, although we knew there was no escape... because we were hetero-sexuals, and we'd always find ourselves under some man.

Before long I grew to like Ania so much, I started inviting her into my sessions, for tips. She'd leave with cigarette money, or a little more, and it was only a question of time before she was "on the floor" with us, the whores. What a sight she was with her white Lithuanian skin, her bleached blonde hair, those long legs, and God, tattoos on each arm. On one arm, a sexy woman, posing in a tiny bikini. On the other arm, a sexy man, posing likewise in a sexy bikini. Large tattoos, covering almost each upper arm. Good detail and shading, and lots of pastel colors.

Over the years I watched Ania's tattoos lose their clarity somewhat, but good tattoos will almost always stay good — they just change. There's a sort of metaphor inherent in tattooing — nothing certainly is permanent. You'll live with it until you die, but you will die. "This too, shall pass." Accepting the imperma-nence of all things and all situations can cause a person to end up in places like 23rd Street, working as a sleazy whore. The ends jus-tify the means, but the ends have no permanence; therefore, any judgement of the means becomes quite meaningless.

Yes, you are a sleazy whore, but you will probably eat well that day, go home in a cab, and wake up the next day, pay your phone bill, and on your way home, sit in Washington Square Park for half an hour, buy a little of some drug you haven't tried much, yet, and still have enough cash left over to wander in Balducci's guilt-ridden, and buy something wonderful to cook for dinner, probably picking up a Spanish melon to give to the old single man who lives in the apartment next door, who looks like he could use some fresh fruit. Shit, it's probably been years since he had a Spanish melon, and maybe he's never had one. And after you've given it to him, and he's thanked you, you go away, with your Balducci's bag of unnecessary alimentary indulgences, and you're thinking only about that new drug and which video you're going to look at while you consume it ("Videodrome") and you honestly believe the old man doesn't know you're nothing but a sleazy whore.

"Thank God there are whores living here," the old man thinks while he eats his melon. He doesn't actually need the melon, he's eaten a cheap apple every day on his late doctor's orders for the past forty years, but he's watching the television news while he eats, and there's a recession raging, and whores like his neighbor are certainly helping the economy with their undeclared tax-free earnings, and their "marginal propensity to save."

The old man was a research analyst on Broad Street for 42 years. His employer fucked him over, and his kids are long-gone and barely even bother with a card on the High Holy Days, and he can't point a finger at a neighbor because she's fucking the system, and God knows, he thought he had been living a "decent" life and was, he thought, better than "her kind..." And now, although he really didn't need that offered melon, he'd certainly taken it, and had watched her ass jiggle as she walked away on those stiletto-heeled mules and heavy Balducci's bags swinging from each tattooed arm, into her little studio apartment... and he envied her.

She didn't seem to care a whit about what her family thought about her profession. She'd been, I learned many years later, a street whore at the age of 12, complete with a couple of Italian pimps she'd delighted in taking advantage of. I thought I knew almost everything about Ania after 15 years, but recently, while doing a four-hour session with Irwin, her best slave, she'd decided to tell us about how she'd come to enter to world of prostitution. Irwin and I had been smoking dope with Ania and we were well into a bottle of Absolut, but suddenly, we were very alert, because Ania had chosen to tell us of her origins, and we had no idea about her "wonder years."

She told us she'd been in Junior High School in Middle Village, and she'd decided to cut school one day and hang out in the East Village, in Manhattan. It wasn't 20 minutes before a couple of pimps spotted her and were laying down their rap. "I can't believe this," thought the prepubescent Ania. "These Dagos are actually wasting their money buying me a meal, and trying to TURN ME OUT!" She'd decided to have some fun with them, and since she knew she would, ultimately, end up back in Middle Village with her family and would have to answer to the school truant officer, she decided to play the situation for whatever it was worth.

She acted excited at the prospect of turning tricks for these two guys, and after a large lunch, she told them, very firmly, that if she was going to be their whore, she'd need to look the part, and that she was, at the very least, in need of a new makeup kit. Somewhat reluctantly, they agreed, and took her to one of the big department stores in Manhattan, such as Saks or Bloomingdale's. There, she allowed the sales help to show her all the latest in cosmetics, and she took one of almost everything. The sales help, smelling a good commission, quickly fell into doing their sales raps, and little Ania was a willing customer.

Soon, the pimps started to argue. "Why do you need four different mascaras?" they'd ask, watching the tabs mount.

"Are you kidding?" retorted little Ania, in her loud, crude, Middle Village accent. "You want me to look good, HUH?!"

"Yeah, of course," they responded, probably growing nervous at the attention their underage protegée was attracting on the sales floor.

"Well, then," she'd go on, "I NEED the four fucking mascaras, OKAY? HUH? OKAY?"

"Yeah, yeah, sure," they muttered, and gave in.

Ania "worked" her "marks" for more than two months that way, demanding clothes, records, large meals, and even drugs, and almost always getting them.

"Did you turn many tricks for them?" I asked.

"Oh, yeah," Ania answered, inhaling deeply and passing me the joint, while readjusting the clothespins on Irwin's balls and nipples. "And I was hardly ever on no fuckin' street corner, neither!" She paused, adjusting Irwin's latex hood. She exhaled loudly and poured herself another vodka. "Those pimps had me working for steady customers." (She pronounced "customers" as "CUSTOMAHS").

"I went to see the same ugly old men, and I fucked them. I never saw no money change hands, so I had to keep after those stupid pimps to keep buying me stuff. Usually they put up wi' my shit, 'cause they had a little twelve-year old ho' to send around, and THEY knew the value of my ass!" she chuckled. I looked at Irwin, and couldn't see his expression, because of the latex hood, but his eyes were wide, and I could tell he was as shocked by this story as I was.

"Did you know this about Ania?" I asked Irwin.

"No," he answered, "and I've known her for more than ten years." I was laughing and Ania was busy rolling another joint. I was so absorbed in the story, I'd forgotten to check the video camera. Possibly all this was recorded. I'll never know. Ania put a latex ball gag into Irwin's mouth, handed me the pump and encouraged me to squeeze it, to inflate the ball in Irwin's mouth. I did so, checking his hood to make sure that his nostrils remained unobstructed. He was such a good slave, he often lapsed into unconsciousness before begging, "Mercy, Mistress!" A bona fide nut — but then, who am I to point a finger?

Finally, Ania told us, she'd figured she'd taken that pimp situation to the max, and she'd retreated to her family's home in Queens, much to the unhappiness of her sleazy employers. For several weeks they tried to track her down, and finally, getting her parents' phone number, they took to calling the house, trying to speak to their errant little piece of underage ass. One day, in exasperation, Ania's mother, having fully grasped the situation, shouted into the phone, "Dat girl is twelve years old! I'm gonna have youse all ARRESTED!" This blunt tactic proved effective, for the hapless pimps ceased their calling and Ania returned, for a time, to he rich fruits of the straight life in Catholic School in Queens.

Ania returned, I suppose, to the Catholic school where she knew Rowan, and rebelled from the nuns like all good Catholic girls. I don't know whether Ania graduated or not, but Rowan graduated only because, she claimed, the nuns felt sorry for her. Rowan's father, an electrician, had never paid income taxes, and the prospect of an IRS audit finally rendered him dead one overcast weekday at the family kitchen table. The nuns at school felt so bad for Rowan, they passed her with straight Ds.

Ania's family probably knew such crisis. One day, Ania revealed to me that she'd been sexually abused by her father. "Why, that's horrible," I said, not really knowing how to respond.

"Nah, my whole family, we're all in therapy," Ania said, "and anyway, I don't remember nothin'. It fucked wi' my sistuh's head worse than it did with mine. I remember my father'd pick me up and hold me when I was about four, and my older sister'd get REAL upset! `Stop that!' she'd order him."

And the father would, guiltily, put little Ania down, and cease to fondle her. Ania said she didn't have any clear memories of an actual sex act with her father, but she was aware of his arousal, and his "special affection" just for her, among all the children of that large family. Eventually he died. Ania liked to wear her blonde hair in a sort of Louise Brooksish bob, and had the look of a wide-eyed silent film actress. "I love gangsters," she told us one day on 23rd Street, pronouncing "gangsters" as "GANGSTAHS." "I think I was a gun moll in my past life," she continued. Her goal was to find herself a gangster, and to be his "squeeze." What she found was Paco, a low-level thief from Staten Island.

Paco was the boyfriend of Itsy, one of the whores on 23rd Street. Ania set her sights on Paco — Itsy-be-damned! Paco's sister, Rosita, came to work with us on 23rd Street as a dominatrix, and quickly, Ania and Rosita became fast friends, united in a wild and sleazy war against Itsy, who disappeared quickly from 23rd Street, but not without demanding the return of her "leopard underwear" from Rosita. "She wants her fuckin' leopard underwear," Rosita snorted, chugging a beer in the whores' "waiting room" on 23rd Street.

"Yeah," sneered Ania, "an' she's complainin' about those leopard shoes she bought Paco!"

Paco shifted his alliance to Ania and went to live with her, his own family's house being off-limits to him after he'd stolen and sold his mother's antique jewelry, the silverware, and everything else he could fence. "That Paco is no damned good," mused Rosita one day, yet she seemed largely unconcerned with the pain he'd inflicted on his family, a lower middle class, hardworking Portuguese clan who were not, themselves, entirely without guilt when it came to having light fingers. (Rosita would often show up on 23rd Street with boxes of merchandise for us to take — deodorants, cat food, cheap perfumes, etc. The father was, I gathered, a crooked driver or "lumper" somewhere in the city.)

Ania quickly learned the ropes on 23rd Street and became a switchable whore — she could do both dominant and submissive sessions and was one of the top moneymakers in Jack's dubious "stable" Because she'd done her first sessions with me, as mentor, her style was similar to mine — friendly, gentle, making almost everything a game. My own slaves were very loyal — they knew I was basically a happy person, out mostly for a bit of a twisted thrill and grocery money. Ania was no dummy — she'd booked me solid on nights when the other whores had sat idle, wondering why my fat white butt was so damned popular. She copied, at first, my style, and to this day, pulls in a nice piece of change each week. I like to think I helped to train her in the sleazy arts.

She and Paco became commonlaw spouses, unable to actually marry, because Ania was on public assistance, and was getting a monthly Welfare check, food stamps, and medical coverage. After years of working in dusty whorebunkers, Ania developed asthma, and is now seriously ill. She's completely dependent on Uncles Sam's free health insurance. What a twisted system, in the USA. A working whore is unable to get straight medical insurance, both for the fact that she has no acceptable "legal" means of support, and also, that she now has a "preexisting condition" and is uninsurable at this point.

I "retired" from whoredom in 1984. A year later, Ania, Rosita, and Paco came to a party I was having in my Brooklyn apartment. Ania was thin, and she had let her bleached blonde hair grow long. She was a dead ringer for Debbie Harry, but was so hollow-cheeked, I feared she might have AIDS. This wasn't the case, but, like me, she'd found "The Life" a dreadful strain on her immune system, and had begun a slow but definite physical decline. I saw Ania again in the first part of 1993. She was still working for Jack, but the enterprise had relocated to 38th Street in Chelsea, the new street for the kinky brothels in New York. I was still a Wall Street secretary, still dabbling in freelance journalism, and a French magazine had hired me to interview Ania. What a strange feeling, seeing some of my co-workers from a decade earlier, still plying their kinky trade. It was as if time had almost stood still.

But Ania didn't look good. She was too thin, and was smoking pot and drinking too much. Often, her answers to my question were completely unrelated to what I'd asked. But her technique as a Mistress had blossomed. She had an enormous metal trunk, absolutely packed with strange implements. She had everything out and scattered around the sleazy, windowless room, which was cold and smelled bad.

About six months later, I left my second husband and returned to The Life. Of course, my first choice for places to work was 28th Street, with Ania. She'd gained weight, and was sexier than ever. We spent a lot of time in her room, smoking joints and talking about everything. One night, we'd smoked a lot, and I was heavily into a bottle of champagne. "Let me give you a massage, Mistress!" I quipped, pushed her face down, onto her sleazy bed. I began to massage her, and she protested only lightly, being as stoned as I was. "Oh, Mistress, what a lovely ass!" I screamed, and pulled up her miniskirt, exposing twin spheres of soft, white butt-flesh.

"Stop!" she giggled, as I started to kiss her ass.

"What, Mistress?" I asked, pretending not to understand her. I turned her over and lunged for her pussy, thrusting my tongue deep inside. She yielded for several minutes although complaining halfheartedly about the assault.

I had a taste of cunt I hadn't experienced in years, being long-retired, and only sometimes bisexual. I was wearing bright red whore lipstick, and began to tickle her and plant red kissmarks on her thighs and butt, above the tops of her black, sheer stockings. She got up, and staggered to the waiting room area, where she sat in the phonegirl's chair, trying to occupy herself with her former role as receptionist, but I wouldn't leave her alone. I threw myself onto the dirty floor, at her feet, and began tongue-cleaning her shoes. "I love you, Mistress!" I chanted.

"Stop!" she kept screaming, amid laughter, but doing nothing to actually stop me. Finally, she teetered into one of the little fuckrooms where the rest of the whores were lounging (it was the warmest room in the place), probably hiding from us. "Look what she did to me," Ania wailed to them, pointing at her kiss-bedecked white flesh. I remained on the floor, watching TV and chuckling to myself. Ania's cunt tasted so good.

5. *Montescudaio, Italy*

I always had a fascination with Italy. My family's neighbors in Ohio were from Calabria. They pressed their own wine and made their own pasta, hanging it up on the clothesline in the basement to dry. My mother said, "Can my daughter come watch?" Mom was setting me firmly on a course of Italian-loving ways. When they pressed the wine, the unfermented juice was called "moussht."

"You like?" the old men said, giving me glass after glass.

"Yes," I replied.

"You drink enough, you go to toilet all day," they chanted and chuckled.

At my request, photos were taken of me in a bombed-out villa, which was being used as the art space of tiny Etruscan town's sole artist, Steffano Tonnelli, who'd invited me (as BIKINI GIRL) and Vittore Baroni (as self-publishing mail artist) to be guests of Montescudaio, Italy, for the day. For the photos I wanted taken in the dramatic setting of the destroyed villa, I was handcuffed to an old door and left to sit like that a long time before the photo was taken, so that I would be realistically drooping with fatigue when the shutter finally snapped. It was a gift, for Fred, "The Professor", of course, back in the States, that photo. That was just the sort of pose he liked.

Montescudaio is near Pisa, but is not found on most maps. Vittore drove us around the countryside for a couple of hours — no one had heard of the town. Finally, one peasant pointed up. There, at the top of a rocky mount, we thought we saw a building. We drove a long time up steep, narrow roads until we found Montescudaio, perched near the top of a little mountain.

Fabulous views of the surrounding countryside below, but walking down the town's few tiny, steep little cobble-stoned streets, you felt like you were going to fall off and go tumbling down the cliffs. The town has one old church, some stone cottages, no stores that I can recall (there must have been one, but no one put up a sign — everyone just knew where the store was), and one restaurant, called La Contessa, which also had no sign on it — again, everyone just knew it's there. Everything in Montescudaio seemed to be on the vertical.

I figured, "Hell, the town is Etruscan — it hasn't fallen off the mountain yet, don't figure it's gonna fall off today," and I tried to relax, but have a slight fear of heights, so remained edgy throughout the visit. The little stone cottages opened right into the streets, and most seemed to have widescreen televisions. Italians love gadgets. They'll cheerfully live in a two-roomed stone cottage, but you'll usually find the latest-model appliances within. Go figure. Maybe that's one of the things I love about Italy. If you have a taste for the absurd, go give it a looksee.

I first studied the Italian language in 1976, in Kent, Ohio, at Kent State. I found the language astonishingly direct and easy. Okay, the verbs were a bitch. But the rest — well, I could do it. I got A's. Always got A's in Italian. B's in French, but A's in Italian. And I eventually fell in love with a French guy and married him! After more than four years of living in France, I can still only read French at a third-grade level. I was fluent in Italian almost right away and was told I spoke with little accent. Oh, well. I wrote home to my parents from Kent State and asked if they could find the money to help me study in Italy. "No way," my father said. So I knew I'd have to do it myself. Heartbroken, I moved to New York, to have my heart broken further by a punk rock singer, and to work as a call girl and bondage model to save up the tuition for the University of Florence — a summer semester, arranged by Brooklyn College.

I worked for a type of "Mayflower Madame", but one who ran a brothel as well as classy out-call. With my simple looks and necklace of real pearls, I always got past hotel security. The clients would open their doors (usually hotel rooms) and just kind of peer at me, in my business suit and brief case. I extended my hand to shake. "I'm from the agency," I said quietly.

"Oh!" they said, snapping out of it. I was always manicured, wore no heavy perfume or makeup, and had beige stockings, a garter belt, and matching pure silk pushup bra and lacy panties. And sensible low-heeled pumps, but of very good leather.

"What's a nice girl like you doing in a job like this?" a guy from Iran, an electrical engineer who had placed his family in Switzerland, said to me.

"Saving up money for a semester of college in Italy," I replied, simply.

"That's nice," he said, lying back, sipping his whiskey. I sipped mine, took a shower before and after our encounter, at his request (I think he was afraid I was not clean) and dressed to leave when it was all over. "What I really need now is a good secretary," he said.

"You're kidding?" I laughed. "I'm a secretary. I have a portable typewriter and everything."

"Could you come back tomorrow at three?" he asked. I said yes, and did, failing to notify the call girl agency who had sent me to the Iranian guy from Switzerland in the first place. (Freelancing is a good way to get killed — but I wanted to help him out, and get the extra cash.)

I sat at his table and wrote a concise business proposal in neat English about an electrical contracting bid he had won for a series of buildings in Switzerland. I had an envelope ready. He signed the neatly typed letter I had composed, based on his dictation in broken English, and I gave it to him to seal and mail. Two one-hundred dollar bills fluttered down onto my keyboard. "This is very generous," I said.

"If only you knew how much money you just made me," he said, smiling broadly. "Here," he said further, gesturing. And he handing me a box of fine French perfume, probably intended for his wife back in Switzerland. "Wow!" was all I could say. I excused myself and went down the street richer, smelling sweeter, and lugging my little portable Olivetti manual back home to Brooklyn.

What kind of parents would not give their honors student daughter the money to study art history and Italian in Italy? Beats me. My father was always very clear — the family could do little to finance my college education. I think my parents were basically mean, and were terribly cheap — they refused to help me with my college education past my first or second year. For the second year, I won a merit scholarship to pay for half the cost of tuition. From then on, I paid for both my undergraduate and graduate school studies myself. Since my parents wouldn't pay for my college education, I had to pay for it myself. Did they really prefer I sell my body in New York to save up to study in Italy? I guess they did. If I ever have a child, I swear, I will give every last penny, will go in debt to the eyeballs, to pay for the education of my child. A child turning tricks to get an education is an abomination. Any way you slice it, it don't look purty.

Vittore Baroni was a mail-artist I had been in touch with via the mail-art network for many years. I wrote and told him I'd be attending the University of Florence, but would be free the month of August. Could I come visit him? He said, yes, but the hotel his family owned on the Italian Riviera was booked solid, so I'd have to share an attic room with his sister, on a cot. I said yes, and was glad to meet the sister. She had no say in it, and did not seem to enjoy my snoring, but she remained stoic and philosophical about sharing her little room with me.

I took my meals in the back of the hotel, with the help. Before each meal, Vittore, who was managing the front desk, would serve me an elegant aperitivo — usually Campari and soda, warm to my American tongue (Europeans do not seem to ice their drinks the way Americans do). Then, we'd head back to the kitchen, and I'd watch the maids, dressed in cute little uniforms, fold the bedsheets and gossip. A large pasta meal was set out, and I gorged myself. After dinner, Vittore would take me driving around the sleepy little resort town, and we'd tour the avenues of Viareggio, unburned during the war and all wood, Art Deco. Fascinating.

I spent a few days on the fancy beach, not really knowing much what to do with myself, but enjoying the fact that I was getting a tan for free on the Italian Riviera. The sand is white there, too, which is somewhat rare on the Italian Riviera, I understand. (Most of the beaches there are stony.)

I sat up late at nights, talking to Vittore about his mail-art projects. His family had some money. He was pretty much free to do as he pleased. He was losing his hair, though, and felt bad about that. I told him not to worry about it, the right woman wouldn't care. I tried to be that right woman. A few years later he found his "right woman" who didn't care he was balding, married her, built her a house, and they have a son together. Happy endings seem so rare in this Bizarre Life...

In the town of Montescudaio, the day had been declared "visiting artist day." Vittore and I were the only two visiting artists! Steffano Tonnelli had organized it. I showed examples of my magazine, BIKINI GIRL, and gave some away. Vittore did most of the talking, but I could speak a little Italian at the time. Then, Vittore talked about what it means to be a mail-artist, part of a vast network of people connecting through the mail. We were served a lunch at La Contessa — snails and rabbit, all caught locally. The afternoon was hot and sleepy, and in the bombed-out villa, there was a mattress where we could nap, but I only wanted to curl up with Steffano, who seemed to have been already claimed by some local female who was never far from his side and gave me dirty looks, so I was not to score with him. Thus, Vittore and I sat outside the church in the great heat, and watched the hills of Leonardo da Vinci spread beneath us, told bad jokes, and passed the time.

When evening came, we had a "pop" concert. Vittore gathered everyone in the town — about 60 people — into the main square, and we were all given big wads of bubble gum, which we blew into big bubbles and... popped! I suppose this is performance art. A pop concert — literally! I thanked Vittore for his hospitality, took a bus back to Florence, checked my mail, and visited with "Lo Vecchio", one of my best tricks I'd met there during the summer. He gave me his business card from IBM, and I stayed in touch for a few years. He took me for one long, late night dinner on the river Arno, having them wheel over a cart filled with meats and vegetables, and I just picked whatever I wanted. It was a romantic setting, and the food was delicious and the view of the Arno superb. Then, I went to Venice, all alone, spent one night in a costly place, saw I couldn't afford it, and went back to the little pensione I'd stayed in earlier that summer with my art history class at The University of Florence. A tiny bed with sink, just about $6 a night.

I promised myself I'd see the sights, but instead, I rode the ferry boat to the Lido each day and spent the day on that grungy beach. On my way there, I found a cafeteria that'd sell me a big bowl of soup for fifty cents, so I'd make that bowl of soup my main meal for the day. I'd write letters to Harry Smith and Ondine, back in New York. I only had one book to read, "Popism" by Warhol, so read and reread it. I had enough money for one cold beer at day's end and one bag of chips — heavenly! — then I'd take the ferry back to my room, wipe the sand and salt off myself, and go to the deli and get cheap wine, olives wrapped in paper, greasy bread, and slices of ham. Maybe an apple for dessert. And I could hear the footsteps shuffling beneath my window on the cobblestones, and the church bells, and I always fell asleep early, after my shower in the little communal shower stall in the pensione's hallway. Sunburned skin cooling down after the shower... nature's tranquilizer.

There was a trattoria I liked on Square Saint Tomas nearby. I sat and drank wine and read a book. The owner caught my eye. His name was Pietro, and he also owned an Australian place in town. He was a true Venetian, he assured me — rare. He had lived in Australia many years and spoke excellent English. I sat and slowly devoured his large pizzas and drank while he finished up work — he never paid for this, I had to pay my own way, but the prices were reasonable — then when he was off work, he said, "Come, I'll show you the Venice a tourist can never see." And he'd walk me to mysterious areas I've never found since, in two repeat visits to Venice.

He owned several apartments around town, which he rented to his waiters, and liked to cum on my breasts and smear it into my tit-skin. I found this a good way of getting a free shower, as I'd need to clean up with soap and hot water after he squirted all over me. Years later, I was there in the trattoria Pietro owned with my second husband, and Pietro recognized me and started to come over, but I shook my head and he backed off. Oh, well. So much for Pietro. When I got back to New York, my skin was glossy and golden from three months of olive oil eating and sun. I had my hair permed and plucked my eyebrows. No one recognized me.

6. The Grand Central Of Sleaze

Each day I worked at The Grand Central of Sleaze, I kept my attire simple. The top was given to me by Mistress Ann, who came from a good family in Michigan, and, unknown to me at the time, was the live-in lover who took up with my first husband, Wolfe the Junkie, just after I decamped. Ann had bought the top in Tahiti, where she had gone one weekend when she had been bored. ("It was boring there," she said when I asked her how Tahiti was.)

The top was a shiny punk material and had a diagonal strip of clear plastic running along the front. It showed what little cleavage I had (which wasn't much), but no more. A typical "tease 'em" whore shirt. The motorcycle chain belt was real, and was one of the first gifts I bought for myself (mail-order) when I left home and went away to my first college. The little black leather miniskirt was a staple in my wardrobe for years. I think I still have it somewhere. I wonder how many semen stains are on it? Of course, I wore seamless stockings (I have no objection to seams, but believe that if you don't have the time to make sure they are always kept straight, you shouldn't wear them), held up with a black leather garter belt. My panties were also black leather. They had a detachable crotch — very handy. The shoes were my trademark. The heels are six inches tall. Other women would borrow them and try to walk in them, and couldn't. It's like wearing toe shoes all the time — you have to build up the muscles. Takes strength, balance, and lots of practice.

The room I usually worked in had one source of heat — a very small electric space heater. That little space heater was a real fire hazard, and the place was a firetrap. We had a very rickety central heating and air conditioning system, so we had to run those little space heaters in the rooms where we worked (turned tricks) during the cold New York winters. The room I usually worked in had a stock. It was poorly constructed, too tall for most people, and mostly just for show. Not that anyone cared about props in that place. We, the female flesh, were the props. Sorry props, at that. No one who could work someplace better worked there. Maybe I was an exception, but I was too lazy to look for someplace better to work. I didn't have spectacular looks or a huge collection of "toys", though, so I probably wouldn't have fit in at the "better" places, anyway.

And a lot of people in the biz had a hard time with the fact that I nearly always held down straight jobs. They thought I was WEIRD because I pursued straight money and paid taxes. Cheap plywood pressboard walls. The whole place was "furnished" like that. Some second or thirdhand wall-to-wall carpeting covered the floor. It was so dirty to begin with that it was impossible to ever get clean. Every night the phone girl was supposed to vacuum the place, but the old vacuum cleaner was so tired and worn out, it barely had any suction left in it. (Like most of us who worked there, come to think of it.)

It was around April 1983. I had just been on a one-week vacation to Martinique, alone, to reward myself for getting a straight job as a legal secretary at a bank. I loved the job and my bosses were really nice, but my salary was around $11,000 a year and I had to work at The Grand Central of Sleaze two or three times a week to earn a living. I ended up quitting my job at the bank after only four months. I figured I got the most out of it I could — they taught me word processing, and how to be both a legal stenographer and a paralegal aide. I took my new know-how uptown, and got a job at $18,000 a year as a Mergers and Acquisitions Assistant for an old-money house who fancied themselves American aristocracy, buggered each other on a regular basis (most dying a few years later of AIDS), and did leveraged buyouts and sale-lease-backs. I saw no reason to quit my job at The Grand Central of Sleaze — anyway, I still couldn't stretch $18,000 a year to live on. And I had a rent-stabilized apartment in Brooklyn. Remember, these were already the Eighties. It took a lot just to tread water in New York City.

One fun aspect of being a kinky hooker was that sometimes I'd recognize co-workers or business types from the street. It was fun, seeing them strutting around importantly with their suits and briefcases and portable phones (which were, at the time, a novelty) during the day, then having them show up and "pick" me out of a line of tired whores, and let me lead them into a dusty cubicle where I'd whip their pasty asses. I think some men in the office buildings I worked in recognized me from peep show loops and even from The Grand Central of Sleaze, but they just stared at me, and I stared back, smiling. What could they say?

I did have a nasty shock, once. It was late one cold winter night, and a tourist client from Wisconsin came in. He looked at me, startled. "I recognize you! You're Lisa!" Shit! He knew my real name! (My working names were either Elizabeth, when I was dom, or Lila, when I was sub.)

"Yeah, that's my name all right," I replied glumly. "How did you know?"

"Oh, you did this great 60minute movie, `The Lady of the House', and I remember your name from the credits." Shit! I had done one semi-porn, kinky shot-on-video movie for Esoteric Press in the early Eighties, and those thoughtless fools had put my real name on the box. I prayed no one would ever see it, but that thought was foolish. One thing you have to know for sure in the sex world is that once you enter it, everyone back home is going to find out, sooner or later. Probably sooner.

I also referred to The Grand Central of Sleaze as "23rd Street", because that was where it was located. Around 23rd and 3rd, in the late 1970s and early 1980s, most of New York's S/M whorehouses were located there. I don't know why, but I have my suspicions. It was kind of funny, because you'd often see domina-trixes in full costume walking out in the street, going for fancy ice cream to binge on (most of us were potheads). They'd been just too lazy to change their clothes in order to run out for a snack. One problem was that, of course, many of them were hardcore drug addicts, so they'd beg to go out for "a slice of pizza" and quickly jump in a cab and run somewhere to score some hard drugs, hoping to make it back to work in 15 or 20 minutes so the boss didn't notice. But they would instead disappear for hours at a time, missing their appointments, and the boss where I worked soon kept us locked up for 5 to 12 hour stretches at a time.

There were no windows in the place, of course, and we all went totally batty, cooped up there together for our long shifts, chatting and arguing between tricks, and then spending hour-long sessions at sixty bucks a pop and no tipping with the real tightwads of New York whore clientele. For awhile, though, it was fun, whore-watching around 23rd and 3rd. You'd see tall Mistresses teetering about on needle heels, chains hanging from their catsuits, standing calmly in line at the Kentucky Fried Chicken.

If you were very cheap and just a voyeur, you could hang out in one of the local bars, such as Molly Malone's or Ye Auld Sod, and peek out the front window and watch the prostitutes walk by. Some of the professional slave girls were heavily pierced and tattooed, back before this was so mainstream and popular, and they often had purple hair and matching purple leather costumes.

23rd Street was owned by someone I knew only as Al. Rumor had it he had fallen in love with Tina, a kinky whore, and she had "turned him out" — encouraged him to enter the world of

kinky sex and pimping. She insisted he use funds from his legitimate business — a chain of hardware stores, I think — to set up a
series of bottom-of-the-barrel knocking shops. Tina stayed at
home with their child, Aubrey, and played housewife while Al ran
his legitimate businesses and kept in touch with us by carphone. I
saw very little of him. He was tall, fairly good looking, and dressed
often in brown polyester. Remember the saying? A gentleman
never wears brown. That applied for sure to Al. He was never
openly abusive with us, but he administered strict and generally
nonsensical rules via his phone girls while he was driving around
in his car, using his mobile telephone.

Each of his houses had a "hawkeye", who was a male flunky
who was supposed to protect us, but who generally only ran out to
get us growlers of matzoh ball soup and serve as a drug connection.
Al ran a series of ads in SCREW magazine, all showing women
who no longer worked for him, all promising a taste of paradise at
bargain basement prices. And for sure, all you got was the basement. Not much of a bargain!

At 23rd Street, which was located above a beauty parlor,
clients would ring the bell and would talk to the phone girl via
intercom. They'd climb a long, straight, filthy set of stairs (I don't
think I ever knew it to be swept out in two years) and wait at a second door at the top. There, they'd be viewed through a one-way
mirror. If they were black, they were always turned away. No
exceptions. If they looked "funny", they were also turned away.
Plumbing problems were always the excuse given. If they passed

our admittedly highly questionable "muster", they were allowed in and shown a threadbare seat in a windowless, airless waiting room.

No effort was made to keep clients apart or to make them comfortable in any way. If we had a rush, 8 to 10 guys at a time would be crammed into the waiting room and forced to stand and wait. Many put up with this treatment! We whores often wondered if they made eye contact in there; if they chatted; if they just stared at the ceiling? Why did they put up with being treated like this? We offered not even a complimentary glass of cheap wine. The women were called to order, and we tossed on a few dabs of lip-stick and went and stood in a line by the front door. We were pointed out and named by the phone girl, one at a time. If we were being introduced as "slave girls", our submissive names would be used. If we were being introduced as Mistresses, our dominant names would be used. It got quite confusing.

The client would either select, or ask to leave. Sometimes, it was not so easy for the client to leave. "Is there some problem?" he'd be asked. I always waited to hear one say, "Yeah, bitch, the problem is, these women are all dogs," (I probably would have cheered him on), but the clients were generally exceedingly meek. Many were dangerously drunk, too. Once a client picked me, I'd say, "Come with me, please," and escort him to one of our three rooms. I'd say, "Make yourself completely comfortable," and leave at once. I'd return in five minutes, and if he wasn't buck nekkid with the money laid out on the bed, I'd leave until he figured out what he was expected to do. I gave the money — usually sixty dollars for a dominant session — to the phone girl, and the time of my session was noted. It was also noted if he was new, a house regular, or one of my regulars. Thus, we were rated by Al. If we pulled in a lot of personal regulars, we had a better chance of keeping our jobs. (I actually knew a few women in this place who were so down-and-out, Al actually fired them. I mean, you had to be TERRIBLE to get fired from this place!)

Al knew I ran ads in personals magazines and pulled in my own clientele. He had no problem with this, as long as I was very careful. When I saw a contactee was bona fide, I told them the truth — I didn't usually have time to meet new people on my own, for free. I could see them on 23rd Street once, and could possibly see them privately after that. No promises. Al never objected to this, since he always got a take on my first contact. A surprising number of clients said yes and came to see me in that shameful place. Repeat visits, too. I apologized for taking their money, but I did find many good personal slaves this way (a few masters, too) so I think — I hope — it all balanced out. Because when I "took a slave private", I hardly ever charged a fee. There were exceptions to this, of course. More on this in subsequent chapters.

Normally, to "take a trick private" was good cause for getting your legs broken — or much worse, especially in dealing with pimps like Al. But I told Al from the outset what the deal was with me — that I was a swinger and basically straight — and as long as he took his cut, he didn't seem to mind too much. Since I had said from the beginning I would bring in my own business and take responsibility for their actions, and might or might not begin to see them privately, Al really couldn't find much fault with me. Also, to be sure, I was one of his few workers who wasn't into hard drugs. I was already alcoholic, but kept it in check best I could.

I worked for Al from January 1982 until January 1984. I told him I had been saving up for graduate school, which was the truth. My co-workers found it odd and amazing that I was a college girl. Most of my clients did, too, I think. I informed Al a month in advance that I was going to "retire" He wished me luck. One of my clients had fallen deeply in love with me, and cried. He begged me to let him drive me home from my night school class in my M.B.A. program. I agreed, and he did so for about six months. I turned a few tricks with him privately during that time period, but mostly we were just friends. We are still in touch.

One night, he had his face in my ass, and said, "Elizabeth, this will be the last time." And he wept. Either he was too in love with me, or preferred solid prostitutes. I never asked which. The "comfort" of a whorehouse setting was calming to him. No strings. But to see me in my apartment, to drive me home from school and chat, I think that was just too "real" for him. His wife had died of cancer. Her name had been Elizabeth. He raised four kids alone, lived in Staten Island, and worked for the Post Office. He has possibly retired by now. I heard he got cancer but I don't know whether or not to believe that. He is smoke upon mirrors. So am I.

"So, what are you interested in?" I'd always ask, once they had paid. I had transferred the money to the phone girl, and I had returned to find them sitting uncomfortably naked on the flea-bitten bed. "Well, I'm not into pain," they'd usually begin. We working girls would always laugh about that amongst ourselves. If they weren't into pain, what were they doing in an S/M whorehouse? I learned to say, "Oh, you want it light, right? A fantasy? No marks?"

"Yes," they'd always reply, relieved. It was like seeing the same guy over and over.

"Well, don't worry," I'd say. "I'm very gentle and this is just a game to me. I'm into this only to a point. I don't need to make you cry to get my rocks off, okay? Besides, you'd only drop a dime on me if I roughed you up." "Dropping a dime" was one of the only things that scared us. That meant that if a trick got annoyed about something we did, he'd leave, go straight to a payphone, call the police, and report what we were doing. It didn't happen very often — we tried to be very, very nice to the tricks (to the extent possible) — but once in awhile, there was a bust. Of course, the police knew we were there. They may have even been getting paid off — I don't know.

I came out of the toilet one day and walked smack into the front of a huge cop. He looked me up and down and walked away. Bewildered, I found the place overrun with uniformed police. "This isn't a shakedown," one of them told us. "We just wanna get a couple of girls and get laid."

"Oh, um, this isn't a straight whorehouse," our valiant phone girl said. "Our straight whorehouse is on 24th Street. I'll give you the phone number. Call them up and tell them what you want, and they'll accommodate you, officers." Spanky, our phone girl (I think that was really her name!) then recited the phone number of our 24th Street house (which catered to very old men, but that's another story), and got it wrong by one digit. The police noted it and left.

"Why did you give out the wrong phone number?" I asked, incredulous.

"I doubt they are even gonna call," she said, "but this way, if they do and find I gave them a bum steer and they come back to hassle me, I can just say I was so damned nervous, I got the number wrong by one digit, that's all." I had to admit, she was clever.

"Do you think they'll really call?" I asked.

"Nah," she replied, taking a pull from a tequila bottle she kept hidden under her seat cushion. "Face it — those cops don't want one of our skanky 24th Street whores. They were just up here checking us out, probably."

We did get busted for real from time to time, though. I was never there when it happened — I only worked there part-time. Getting busted was a hazard borne by our full-time crew. One night, Szandora, one of our sweetest and most fucked-up workers, who later died of AIDS, called out in a strange voice, "Spanky? SPANKY?" I heard this story secondhand, from Ania. Apparently, Szandora had foolishly discussed a submissive sex act with a plain-clothes cop before he was buck nekkid and before she had asked him, "Are you a cop?" See, if we asked them directly if they were cops and they said no, they couldn't proceed with a bust, because then that would be entrapment. Of course, it would be our word against theirs, although our word wouldn't hold up in a court where the judge wanted us to take a fall no matter what. But, basically, that was the law in New York State.

Szandora had gotten us busted, poor girl. She was really scared. Not of being busted per se, but of being cut off from her drug supply for a few days. She had a mean habit — she injected various things. Ania said she heard the bust going down through the thin walls and said to her client calmly, "Just get dressed, honey, real fast, and sit here on the bed with me. They don't want you — you're gonna walk." The client, all ajitter, put on his clothes, they sat down on the bed, and sure enough, the door flew open. "This is a bust!"

"Officer, there must be some misunderstanding," Ania said in her thick Queens accent. "My friend and I, we ain't doin' nothin' but talkin'. He just come by to visit me is all." The cop glared at her, blood in his eye. He knew she'd outsmarted him. There was no evidence of any actual illegal activity going on. He asked for her i.d. and the i.d. of the client, then, very very reluctantly, told them both to get lost. The client was gone in a flash, and Ania packed up quickly and went home.

Szandora spent the night in jail, along with Spanky, but the other girls were released after being detained and questioned awhile They all played dumb and acted as polite as they could toward the police. Al had to bail out his two co-workers, pay fines, arrange pay-offs probably, and we had to shut down for a few days. But a few days later, it was business as usual.

Everyone was always extra-skittish after a bust, naturally. I remained philosophical about it. I had a clean record and knew the worst that could happen was that I'd spend a holiday weekend on Riker's Island (which I've heard is hell on Earth), and the charges would probably eventually be dropped, anyway. We began to have an escalating problem with busts and fuck-ups on 23rd Street, and I knew for sure it was time to retire. We even had a bomb once — someone threw it at the front of our building. All it did was shatter the windows in the beauty parlor next to the hardware store downstairs from us, but apparently and understandably, it scared the shit out of the few remaining girls who were still turning tricks there. One night, someone broke in and smashed all our plumbing. The hardware store downstairs was flooded, and Al had to pay for all the repairs. The vibe got increasingly bad on 23rd Street. My last month of working there, we moved to around 27th Street and Avenue of the Americas. I'll refer to it as "27th Street." I'm not even sure exactly where the building was — it's not even there anymore, it's a parking lot or something now.

The new facilities were on the top two floors of a crumbling tenement, and were fairly plush by 23rd Street standards. Al revamped our ads in SCREW, and all of a sudden, business was really booming. One day, I made $1,000. Ania was regularly making $2,000 and $3,000 in a "double shift." I chatted with Sueda one day. "I'm gonna retire at the end of this month," I told her.

"Really? Me too!" Her eyes were wide.

"Yeah, the vibe here isn't good. Do you feel it?"

"Definitely," she replied. "I'm gonna git while the gittin' is good," I continued. "I've been saving up for graduate school. I'm gonna get an M.B.A. and continue on with my straight job." (I was about to go into junk bonds for a few years.)

"Good for you," she said. "I'm gonna get a straight job again in the fashion industry."

We both quit a week before a Super Big Bust. I heard about it a few months later from Ania. She said it had been a horror. Dozens, literally dozens, of cops stormed the place, brandishing sticks and roughing up the girls needlessly. Clemmie, one of our phone girls, escaped, and they chased her down Avenue of the Americas, and dragged her back by the hair to 27th Street, to be tossed into a police truck and hauled off for processing. Another of our women, who was an illegal immigrant from Australia and called herself Violet, was detained for nearly two weeks and deported! I heard bits and pieces of facts about the bust from former co-workers and clients I'd stayed in touch with. It sounded really ugly. 27th Street closed for good. Actually, it just moved around the corner to 28th Street, and I went back to work there about nine years later. But that's another story.

7. *Girl For Hire*

I own hundreds of photos of myself in bondage. Whenever possible, after I've posed in bondage for a photographer, I ask for a set of prints, as a gift afterward. In some cases, I even own the negatives. (Some collectors are so paranoid, they take the photos of me, jerk off to them — I guess! — and then give me back the negatives, for fear their families will discover their dirty little secrets. Then, I think they destroy the prints! In fact, I have one client who I know for a fact burned his photos of me after he jerked off to them.)

In the early 1980s, I met a client, Jim, through a personals ad I ran in a kinky magazine, advertising myself as a bondage model for hire. As you can well imagine, it is very dangerous to write to people, tell them about yourself, and invite them to your house to tie you up and take photos of you. I usually maintained each piece of correspondence for some time before I made a decision about each potential client. I often asked for their work number, but seldom verified anything. I tended to throw caution — cautiously — to the wind. I could usually detect a willingness to be honest, an inherent honesty, in the "good" letters.

These "good" clients turned out to be very steady and generous. I was only paid about $100 for a typical session for generally asked for a bit more for car fare, stockings or special props, etc. I usually borrowed an apartment in the building in which I actually resided, and claimed it was mine. The person whose apartment it was, porn actor Alan Adrian, got a small cash tip for use of his place, and I usually asked for small gifts in addition to the modeling fee and extras, such as a bottle of my favorite whiskey (Wild Turkey, low proof), even some Chinese takeout, delivered during our session, so we could have a snack of steamed dumplings, one of my favorite foods.

The clients were charged a very fair price for my bondage modeling services, so never objected to paying a little extra. The same as on 23rd Street, I kept my prices low and fair and didn't hustle. A repeat customer is a whore's best friend. I did get some very, very scary letters at my P.O. box over the years. And a lot of hilarious ones. One guy named Bob wrote to me from Ohio (where I was born and raised) and said that if I was to be his slave, I would have to quit my job in New York City, drop everything, give up my friends, and move to Ohio and live in his garage. As proof, he sent a photo of himself, naked, in said garage, which had been converted to a dungeon. Scary! I laughed my ass off, and wrote back and thanked him for his letter and returned his photo. I said I was born and raised in Ohio and that for me, it was Hell on Earth, and that no way was I going to submit to being his slave in that wretched place. I mean, my masochism only goes just so far! OHIO!?

One guy in Michigan pressed so hard on the notebook paper he wrote on, his pen nearly pierced the page. He asked how DARE I attempt to set the terms of my slavery to him?!!! The photo he sent of himself was really scary. He was totally encased in a body suit of black leather, all zipped up. There was a little case for his penis. He looked like one of those Mexican wrestling heroes, but done up in black leather! One of my favorite repeat private clients, Jim, lived somewhere in Connecticut and was always punctual and reliable. He loved "damsel in distress" photos, and favored posing me in the act of wriggling toward the telephone, as if I hoped I could somehow dial it with my nose or something. He liked the fact that I was a real-life secretary, and he always asked me to wear my "real" clothes during our modeling sessions. He sure was easy to please!

The bondage was very real, and he was good at it. The gags were effective. He was always careful not to bruise my skin, which tears easily. (A real setback for a bondage model.) I was only tied up for about ten or 20 minutes for each session. Then, I'd be completely untied, change my clothes, and we'd try a different scenario. Just so you know for sure, it is extremely dangerous — even fatal — to be put in bondage in any one position for more than about 20 minutes. The muscles begin to atrophy quickly. Don't listen to any heroic stories about how such and such a model was so good, she could be tied up for two or three hours at a time. If anyone is telling you that and is not lying, they are probably a murderer. Or has seriously injured someone.

Jim would always contact me by mail. We'd arrange a meeting well in advance, usually in connection with one of his business
trips to New York. He really appreciated that I had my friend's
apartment to borrow for our sessions. The last time I saw him was
around 1986 or 1987. He was staying at the Grand Central Hyatt,
where he'd attended a business seminar for the week. He was with
a friend, who was also an enthusiast for kinky photos. He contacted me and asked me if I would pose for two men at one time. I said
sure, just double the fee.

I went up to their hotel room, and asked if I could order a
double Wild Turkey whiskey from room service, to loosen myself
up. They said sure, but since they had officially checked out,
they'd have to pay cash for it. They called the front desk and said
they were still packing and needed a little more time in the room,
and could they have a double whiskey in the meantime? We kept
our friendly chatter to a minimum. I dressed quickly and in no
time, they had me tightly bound on the hotel bed and were snapping away. Unfortunately, all three of us forgot we had ordered
from room service. There was a knock at the door. "Just a
minute!" Jim said. I was not only in full bondage at this point, I
was tied to the bed, which was right in front of the door. In about
two minutes, they loosened the knots and were about to carry me
to the next room and place me on a couch. I was completely
hogtied, so there was no question of untying me further — that
would have taken five minutes more. By this time, the room service guy was very suspicious, and used his pass key to enter, just in

time to see me hopping, on six inch heels, bound and gagged, into the adjacent sitting room.

He left the whiskey, my clients paid and tipped him, I had a drink, we all heaved a sigh of relief, and we got back to the photography. But the room service guy had notified hotel security, of course. Ten minutes later, there was another knock on the door. This time, it was a very tall, very dark African American man in a uniform. He was exceedingly polite, and asked in a deep voice if he could enter. My clients said yes. By this time, I had been untied, but I was dressed in sexy underwear. I said hi to the security guard and assured him everything was okay — I wasn't in any danger. "We're just playing," I said. He rolled his eyes. He asked to see all our identification. I calmly looked through my purse and took out my employee i.d. for the brokerage firm where I was working as a Research Assistant for the Corporate Bond Analyst, at the time. It was a photo i.d. and the guard could clearly see I was just some kinky secretary. The other two showed their i.d.s with shaking hands, their cool completely shattered. They probably were having visions of their employers and families being notified of the incident. "We're leaving shortly, sir," I told the security guard. "I just came to help them pack and to say goodbye." He rolled his eyes again.

"Okay," he said slowly, and left the room, but when we looked through the peephole, we saw he had stationed himself outside our door. He wasn't leaving until we did. Uhoh!

"He's still out there," I informed Jim and his friend, who then really began to panic. "Hey, calm down!" I tried to assure them. "Let's finish our photo session and then calmly leave. We're not really breaking any major laws." But Jim and his friend were thoroughly rattled, untied me, told me to dress, and really did finish their packing. I was paid, with shaking, sweaty hands. "You guys are like two school boys who got caught with a girlie magazine!" I chided them, but there was no calming them down — the session was over. I thanked them, straightened my clothes, opened the door, and proceeded to the front entrance of the hotel, on 42nd Street. I was very aware of the security guard, following me at "a discreet distance" As soon as I hit the street, I turned to him, smiled, waved, and said, "Thank you! Have a nice day!" His face fell. He really thought he'd been silently, expertly tailing me! I never heard from Jim again. One of my best clients, frightened by a hotel rent-a-cop. So it goes.

8. *Chateau 19 and Other Hangouts*

Chateau 19 was on West 19th Street in Manhattan. I think La Marquise was the person who first took me there, so this would be, perhaps, 1979. Sometimes some of the patrons were very famous people. La Marquise, her beleaguered favorite slave, and I were doing an S/M scene out on the small stage the club had provided, and the club clients were sitting back, relaxing, and enjoying the free show. The mood was a little tense — the kind of tension that comes from too much Alice Cooper music and cocaine. (The Club owner, who called himself "Bob" and wore a necklace of human bones, liked to play Alice Cooper's "Killer" album a lot during club hours. It's a great album, but after the 30th time, it kind of grates.)

It wasn't that unusual to see super-celebrities in this small S/M dive. I mean, Oscar winners and such. I had just missed Liza Minnelli there, one night, I heard upon arrival. In the late 1970s in New York, bisexuality and kinky sex were very chic. Everyone looked on, calmly. I am not saying everyone participated, but it was a very decadent, freewheeling atmosphere. As the years passed, Chateau 19 eventually closed, and later, I read in a book called "New York Confidential" that the club had been involved in some very, very sleazy side-businesses, but I never saw any such things while I was there.

I was seldom charged a cover fee — I don't even think there was one for single females. If there was, it was very inexpensive. Drinks were generous, were usually served in plastic cups, and there was a small cocktail lounge up front where you could sit back in little couches and meet other kinky people. I met some nice couples here, some who later opened their own S/M businesses. There was lots of swinging going on. You might very well end up going home for the night with some married couple you'd just met; or, more likely, you'd hear about a private party being held in the next week or so. There was a lot of networking. Generally, things were relaxed and positive. Few people were there to be show-offs or to make a big splash. They just wanted to dress up, have a drink and a toot, sit back, watch a few consensual S/M scenes performed by fellow patrons, and maybe hook up with some new kinky contacts.

The way I dressed to go to Chateau 19 was often the way I went dressed to my secretarial job at the avant-guarde film place. My high white leather boots were my pride and joy. I'd gotten them at a substantial discount during my first job in New York at Carrano, the Italian shoe and handbag designer. I worked for the shoe store boutique chain for about a year. My leather jeans were without lining, and really did fit like a glove. I got them from a little boutique on Lexington Avenue. They cost $125, a fortune to me in those days, but I was charged no tax, as the vendors knew I'd be wearing them in the shoe store and would steer business their way. (I did.)

To get the $125, I had a small speaking part in a 35mm full-length porn movie called "Double Your Pleasure", by Carter Stevens. More on this in another chapter. I found my black leather vest in a Goodwill bin for $2, and usually wore it opened to my navel — not that I had much cleavage to show off. In the New York I knew in the late 1970s, the more punk you dressed, the more likely you were to be left alone on the streets. Criminals tended to go for well-dressed, middle or upper-class types. They knew we punks didn't have much more than cab fare on us; in fact, many of our costumes did not possess pockets! Handbags themselves were a rarity — there were these little pouches called "disco bags" They were slung across your breasts, closed with a draw string, and held your apartment key, paper cash, your stash, and that's about it.

If you needed to adjust your makeup, most of the better discos had a full line of cosmetics and perfumes available for free, along with a bathroom attendant to fetch you Kleenex and help you with your hair between dances (vertical or otherwise). I was always under scrutiny where I lived in the Lower East Side. Only by opening my little handbag wide when I shopped at the bodega, so they could see my purse was almost always empty, did I remain relatively unscathed during the time I lived there. All the local bad guys knew I was just an impoverished punk chick, and wasn't worth their hassling — I had nothing to steal. I even walked around in my underwear and pyjamas on the streets. (Going out in Manhattan often seemed to feel like wandering around in another room of your own apartment.)

Just about the worse thing that ever happened was the local Hispanic guys would spot me and feel a need to voice their approval for my appearance. They'd hiss like snakes at me. "SSSSSsssssssssss!" they'd say. I'd get pissed off and hiss back, or sometimes bark like a dog back at them, or growl, "Suck my cock, maricon!" This usually confused them into submission and silence. The crazier you acted, the more likely you were considered not worth messing with. I sincerely doubt the same strategy would be a good idea these days, but it worked for me then.

Around 1982, I changed my appearance drastically. I began dying my hair light brown, cut it to above shoulder length, wore very mousy glasses, and dressed like my concept of a librarian. Wow, was this a mistake! I looked submissive and available to the wolves, and was often hassled (usually just verbally, thank God) on the streets. Funny (and sad), but the "nice girl" appearance seemed to get me into more trouble than running around looking like a deranged slut.

I often went to Chateau 19 after school and work, usually with La Marquise. Once, we went, and I was wearing a yellowish polyester dress my Mom had just sent from Ohio. (Only a slip underneath, and stockings and garter belt, of course.) La Marquise opened the front of the dress and applied very severe nipple clamps to my breasts, while I had a martini. I paused, to gasp in pain. An appreciative murmur went up among the ogling clients, as I recovered my senses and continued to sip my drink, ignoring the nipple clamps. "How much for your submissive?" people started asking. "Can we rent her for the evening?"

"No way," La Marquise said proudly. "She's all mine." I was 22 years old. Young and wild!

I heard about (but didn't attend) a party at Chateau 19 where five or six nude ladies stood on the bar, along with the selection of alcohols available for cocktails, and had been catheterized. Clients could pick up a tube and have some sterile urine drip directly into their drinks, as either a flavoring agent or a drink in itself. The nude catheterized ladies each drank lots of fluids throughout the evening, in order to be able to provide a steady drip of urinary "flavoring agent."

There were other S/M clubs in New York at the time, to be sure. Some were big, like Hellfire, but others were very fly-by-night and would close after only a month or two. Often, these quickie clubs were very expensive — rather than attempting to build a "real" clientele, the owners were more interested in charging you $5 for a "clean" towel. Kinky clip joints. I remember some of the famous late 1970s sex clubs in New York. The only name that I remember for sure is Plato's Retreat. Plato's was in the Hotel Ansonia and was open most nights. Rates for entry were fair, and entitled one to a dip in a very slimy pool (which I never tried, and I love to swim) and a free buffet, which I also never tried — slimy cold cuts and very tired-looking potato salad. Nonetheless, they usually allowed you to bring your own bottle of alcohol, and charged you only for the "setup" — plastic cups, ice cubes, stirrers, etc. There were "mat rooms" which were empty rooms covered with mats for sex. Rules were posted on the walls. There was a small disco dance floor, complete with revolving mirrored globe.

My favorite of all these sex clubs was down in the Wall Street area, and I cannot for the life of me remember its name. (It may have been "Midnight Interlude") I went there once in late 1978 with pornographer Carter Stevens and several other people, and it was set up with a sort of Roman motif. There was a good sauna, and a clean-looking pool (which I didn't try, but which looked okay) as well as hot whirlpool baths and immaculate showers. A couple of women seemed to be always on-premises. They weren't very attractive, but were extremely friendly. I guess they were employed there to provide sex for clients who hadn't brought a playmate to romp with. (Carter Stevens says this wasn't the case. There were plenty of available ladies to romp with — the club didn't need to hire "staff.")

The main orgy room had drinks and light food available, and most everyone was encouraged to walk around naked, or to use sheets to create "togas", for a Roman effect. Marijuana smoking was definitely allowed — no dealing, but you could bring your own. You could also bring your own coke and pills and such, but again, no dealing was allowed. I suspect each establishment had their house dealers — but I'm guessing. The main room was dark, had thick, fairly clean carpeting, and mats and large cushions to lie upon. I decided to lie back and let five or more men have sex with me at once. One or two cocks in the mouth, a tongue on the pussy, a tongue on each breast, a cock in the cunt, probably someone sucking my toes. No safe sex was used, and I wasn't on the Pill at the time. I just asked everyone not to squirt inside me. A big risk. I had a terrific orgasm. Several people squirted on me. It scares me now to think of the risks I was taking, but back in those times, sex was a very, very casual thing.

I paid nothing to enter this place, and as a young, single, available woman, was usually allowed into most other places for free, as well. That goes for straight places, too, such as Max's Kansas City and Studio 54. I showed up dateless and all dressed up, and managements wisely figured their male (and some female) clientele would spend a lot of money trying to drink me under the table and pick me up, so waived the cover charge in my case. Ha! I have a hollow leg. I usually drank and saw live music for free, like a V.I.P. I very, very seldom let myself be picked up in one of these places. Oh, it did happen sometimes. I met my first husband in Hellfire and married him a week later. But that's another chapter in this Bizarre Life. Maybe.

Home entertainment was very different in New York in the 1970s than from what it is now. People didn't have VCRs, and cable TV was very new and very limited. Rather than go to the trouble and expense of having friends in for a party at your place, it was easier to dress up and go out night clubbing, instead. You'd meet up with your friends at any given club, and party there all night, and not have the mess to worry about cleaning up in the

I was for sale.

dawn. Clubs were generally very open to letting you throw "private parties, by invitation only", and the first two hours of "your" "party" was an open bar for your guests, with reduced bar fees for your guests later in the evening. (You'd generally have to pay a $100 or so fee for this, but that worked out fine for most club owners, as the margins they were making on the drinks later in the evening usually more than made up for the reductions in prices during the open bar and early evening hours. Also, if you think about it, $100 is incredibly cheap for inviting 70 to 80 people you knew to hang out with you and have a good time, and no mess to clean up later. The club did that for you.)

I used to have private parties at Club 57 and The Mudd Club a lot. Often, there was live music, usually provided for free by friends I knew who were in bands (I often did try to cover all their expenses, but generally, they owed me a favor already, so really did play completely for free). I made up cute invitations, often stealing the use of my employer's photocopying machine, and kept my own mailing lists, scrupulously updated. (Sometimes I'd steal use of the employer's postage machine postage. But other times, I'd just buy a roll of stamps and pay for the mailing myself.) As long as I kept prices very low (such as one dollar to get in) and promised an open bar the first two hours of the party and reduced drink prices the rest of the evening, I had places packed and everyone made a nice little profit and had fun.

Most of my friends at the time (and some of my employers) knew I was a bondage model. My kinkiness was not hidden; if anything, it was flaunted. It was certainly accepted by most people — and if they didn't like it, they showed me a phony face and told me it didn't bother them. I can't worry, after all this time, about what they really thought about what I was doing. I tried to focus on what I thought about what I was doing. And generally, I approved of it. Money on the side, some weird kicks, and the constant threat of serious injury.

9. *Penance*

The Professor took at least a thousand photos of me. Some of the poses had been carefully preplanned and props were ready, or else I just "winged it" and Fred would cry out, "Hold it!" I learned to freeze at a moment's notice — even when I was reaching for a glass of sparkling wine. I was, and still am, so used to modeling, I have learned both how to take orders and also to give direction, simultaneously — if I sense a photographer has run out of ideas, I can suggest lighting ideas and poses, very easily.

I got my first job as a model for the Kent State University Art Department in Kent, Ohio in 1975 and kept working for them for a year or so. It was just nude modeling for a bunch of student sketchers, painters and sculptors, but I do recall the first time, disrobing before all those eyes was a rush. I was scared, and it was cold in the classroom. I only earned minimum wage. I was afraid my parents would find out. I used most of the extra money to buy school books and materials, but I also sent away for punk records and magazines, which were all the new rage at the time.

I got several dishwashing jobs on campus, and learned to eat untouched food from discarded plates on the conveyor belt back to the dishwashing area, so I could eat for free. I'd quickly stuff a piece of cake into my mouth when I thought no one was looking. The other dishwashers were doing it, too.

I learned to hold poses for long periods of time, to take orders without question, and to relax and slide quietly into poses I knew were better, when I disagreed with what I was being directed to do. I'd have to sit for 30 to 60 minutes at a time, unless I was doing "action poses", which were five minutes apiece. Fred, "The Professor", was delighted with my modeling abilities. He also liked my body, which was rapidly changing from "little boy" to "real woman", since I'd been raped, had a partial hysterectomy, and been placed on the birth control pill. As my hips spread and flesh appeared on the backs of my legs, he was happily snapping away.

His second wife, who had died of drink, had also felt unhappy about the changes in her figure after her pregnancies and going on the Pill. Fred tried to console her, but it's often a thing a woman just can't accept, the changes in the body after pregnancy or the Pill. Getting a "womanly" body just isn't cool these days. We are expected to be waifs. I was 5'2" at the time and weighed a mere 120 pounds. Yet, I had "meat on my bones" — I was fleshy. I was never the "skinny type" Fred usually posed me in his basement, and liked to show me "weary from hours of corporal punishment and discipline"; in fact, he was extremely kind to me and I seldom had to strike a pose for more than a few minutes at a time. Fred liked to play at spanking and whipping games, and of course only hit me with my advance consent. (We made sound recordings on cassette tape of some of these discipline sessions.)

In most of the pictures, though I look really dejected and tired, the glass of sparkling wine was usually just out of the camera's range, and very much within my reach. I could have, and did, jump up at any given time and yell, "I need to go pee!" or "I want one of those apples for my dessert!" or "I need to roll a joint and smoke it, too bad if you don't like it!"

Fred always said, "Honey, can't you wait just one minute?"

"No!"

"Okay, okay, of course, my dear!" he'd sigh. And thus I was free to run around Fred's house nude, pounding up the stairs, giggling, calling back at him, "You creepy old man!" It was our standing joke, my favorite term of endearment. I loved Fred so much (still do) that it broke my heart, and the only way I could deal with the emotions I was feeling was to call him nasty little names.

Fred was frugal, so between the two of us, we would work in his kitchen for an hour or two, and throw some London broil under the grill, toss up a bibb lettuce salad, have some sparkling wine, cheese and bread, and oh heaven, frozen eclairs. I was "allowed" to have either an entire eclair, along with 20 lashes after dinner (or even before dinner, if I felt up to it), or half the eclair and ten lashes, and the other half with sparkling wine for breakfast, with the remaining stinging 10 lashes given (and these were very real lashes, too) before I'd take the commuter train from Chappaqua down to Grand Central and my day jobs. I had been reimbursed for my return train fare, had a belly full of fine home cooking and had enjoyed hot, steamy baths, a comfy, restful eight hours of sleep, and usually, $80 for my "modeling." (How much of it was posing? How much of it was real?)

I never had the heart to charge Fred more. He was about to retire, and was such a good steady customer and dear friend, the $80 remained our standing price. I even worked for him as a secretary once at that same price. Fred worried about my bare feet on his basement floor, and always had a pair of slippers (his) for me to slip on, and one of his old bathrobes to drape over myself between shots. Usually, I'd take the train from Grand Central to Chappaqua after a day's work in Wall Street. Fred would meet me in his old car, and we'd often shop together at the supermarket for our meal supplies. It was very domestic, felt very cozy to me. He'd take me to his house, quiet now with second wife dead and his kids off to college, we'd set the meat (for the type of meal described above) out to get to room temperature, chill the sparkling wine, and always, always begin with vodka on the rocks. Often, I had some pot to smoke. The curtains were pulled. Fred only worried about the neighbors to a point, but we had to think about their curious kids and such.

After our drinkies, and I had usually had a refreshing bath, down to the basement we'd repair, for several hours of perversion. All to be recorded on photographic film. For what? Well, for me to earn a few extra dollars for, and for Fred, to have something to add to his burgeoning porn collection, and to pull his pud to, I suppose. I dunno. I offered to suck his cock once, and once he let me try. It was not a success. But I'd offered, he'd accepted, and it hadn't worked. So that was that. He never asked and I never offered again. We were both off the hook, sexually. What a relief, really!

Sometimes, while I was kneeling in corners, he'd ask me to keep my head turned, indicating he was going to jerk off. Two minutes later, I'd hear him say, "Okay." This is all I know. I guess he found relief in private, with my back turned. I felt it was not my place to press him further and question him about how, exactly, he was getting his jollies. It was really none of my business.

With clients like Fred, who are good as gold, it never, ever pays to press them to come up with big bucks for a modeling session. They'll pay, all right, but you'll never see them again if you are too pushy about the money thing. Clients like Fred prefer to have a steady "girl" to pose for them, and a fixed price which never waivers over time. I negotiated "extras" from time to time, to compensate me for a rise in the Consumer Price Index. We did a magazine together in 1982 with Hudson Communications, called "Penance and Punishment." It was all photos Fred had taken of me, and we co-wrote the text. I was paid a mere $700, and I think Fred got only his expenses reimbursed (if that!), but he later went on to do a 'zine or two for Harmony. His touch, his artistic signature, is unmistakable. His preference for models: natural blondes if possible, not much makeup, no fancy lingerie. A little more flesh than is fashionable. Most of all, he likes a model with spunk. One who sasses him back, possibly only to receive a few extra lashes with the cane in reply for her naughtiness. One who says, "Screw you, creepy old bastard, I'm tired and I am gonna take a break!"

I WAS FOR SALE.

10. *In Over My Head (Playing Too Rough)*

I still don't know the true identities of that very odd couple. They called themselves, oh, shall we say, "Joe" and "Jane?" One day, while I was visiting them for the purpose of bondage modeling, they went out to run a quick errand and left me alone in the little house in Vermont they were renting. I quickly went through their personal effects, trying to find out who the hell they were. All I found was Jane's driver's license, and it named her as "Jane McAndless, alias" (this is a phony name I am choosing to write this chapter, understand — I never did learn the couple's real names).

There was a very sleazy modeling agency in New York in the '70s whose name I think I'd best not repeat. Maybe it's still around. I don't know. The proprietress was already getting on in years. I never actually met her — we did business through the mail and over the phone. She specialized in models who would do nudity and sex-related work, such as the "Foto Funnies" for NATIONAL LAMPOON magazine. I sent the proprietress an 8 x 10 black and white glossy of myself, and she declared me hired.

The first job she sent me out on (again, all this was done over the phone) was to visit "Jane and Joe" in Vermont, to do some bondage modeling for them. I was to use a prepaid Greyhound bus ticket, and ride for many hours up to New England. The fee was low — somewhere around $150 — and the proprietress was to receive a part of that. I felt I really needed the money (I usually felt desperate for money — a character flaw) so I agreed to the job.

Right from the beginning, there was trouble. I got to the Port Authority Bus Station, and found the ticket hadn't been pre-paid. Instead of turning around and going home, as I should have done, I reached into my wallet and bought a ticket with my own money, one-way, and asked for a receipt. I was doomed, and I had done it to myself. The bus ride was incredibly long — about 10 hours. By the time I got to Vermont, I was exhausted and rumpled. It was already early evening, yet I was to work that night. Joe and Jane (Jane drove — Joe had no license) took me to the little house they were renting. It was in the middle of nowhere I asked for something to eat and a bath before we started work, and was shown the bathroom and given a cold, slightly stale sandwich after I'd freshened up. I sat down to put on my makeup (I used to wear a lot of black eyeliner in those days, and it was tricky to get it right), and they were impatient.

"No, no, forget about that. No one is going to see your eyes," they said. I shrugged, and began applying lipstick. "Forget about that, too. You're going to be gagged. C'mon, hurry up, it's already late," Joe said. Joe was a big guy, with a huge belly, an unkempt beard, and hair that fell in ratted locks nearly to his waist. Jane was slender and very pretty, and I found out later, she often worked as a model herself for Joe, when they couldn't get anyone else to work for them. They both chain-smoked, and seemed very edgy about something. I just couldn't put my finger on it, but something was very wrong with this picture. The rented house was sparsely furnished, but rather nice. The furniture was coarse wood, but Joe had made it himself, and Jane had sewn pretty cushions for it all. Although the house was small, there were many rooms, most unused, since only two people lived there. Joe and Jane were into collecting fetish shoes and clothing, and had one small room up in the eaves completely stuffed with costumes.

I was momentarily distracted, and like a young girl, wanted to play dress-up. Jane relaxed a little. "Yeah, that's what this room is for. You can come in here and pick out a costume any time you want. We like our models to change clothes often." I admired the dress collection, but chose to wear my own lingerie for our warmup photos. I selected a pair of very severe bondage shoes with six-inch heels, electric purple, which buckled onto my feet and then could be secured with tiny locks. I was taken to their bedroom. They didn't have a bed — only a mattress on the floor. "Lie down," Jane commanded. I did so. My wrists were tied, very tightly with white rope behind my back, and cinched. Then, my ankles were tied to my thighs, and each ankle was tied to my wrist. I was completely helpless. Joe and Jane tugged at me to get me in an upright position. "Wow, this bondage is really tight!" I gasped.

"Oh, quit complaining," Joe retorted. "You love it, don't you, bitch?"

Before I could reply, Jane popped one of those golf practice balls — they are hollow and plastic and full of holes — into my mouth, and promptly secured it with thick clear tape, going all around my head, no attention paid to my hair. I began to panic. Would I be able to breathe? Surely, when the tape came off, my hair would be pulled out. I attempted to struggle, but it was quite useless. Jane made sure a few of the holes in the golf ball remained open, so I could still breathe through my mouth, but the ball was hard and painful to my teeth, and I promptly began to drool, unable to swallow properly or close my lips. "That's good," Joe said dreamily, seeing the saliva drip from my mouth.

Jane took a pair of panty hose and pulled one of the legs over my head. The other, she wrapped loosely but securely around my neck. She took a pair of scissors, and cut away the area of the stockings which was around my nostrils, so I could breathe relatively freely through either my nose or my mouth. She continued binding my head with masking tape, pulling the roll of tape around and around. This was too much for me — much too much — and I shook my head in protest. "Stop jiggling around!" she commanded me. "It's too tight!" I tried to say, but all I could do was make choking, mumbling noises.

The LSD began to take effect. I have no idea what possessed me, but I had taken half a hit of acid right after I took my bath. Joe and Jane didn't know I was high, but I was tripping. And in heavy bondage. Why did I do this to myself? I don't know, to this day. I was shaking my head and trying to say, "No, no, no!"

because I wanted them to untie me and take me to the bus station. "Hold your head up," Jane commanded me, as she snapped away with a 35mm camera. "Stick your chest out like a lady!" I complied. Joe had disappeared. After about half an hour of this bondage, Jane untied me, and I lay weeping on the mattress. Joe came back in, and while I was lying down, stuffed his penis in my mouth and quickly squirted into it. I was so high, confused and sore from being tied up, I just swallowed obediently. "That's it," he said softly, wiping his sperm into my torn hair. "Good little slave." I quietly dressed, and Joe and Jane drove me, badly shaken and paid by check (in the future, some of their checks bounced) to the bus terminal, and I rode back to New York.

I posed for Joe and Jane from time to time over the next year or so. Why I kept going back is beyond me. They moved to a bigger house, deeper into the countryside. Their landlord had found out about their bondage photography business, and had evicted them. I used to visit them overnight, sometimes. We had a strange friendship, to say the least. Worse, I introduced them to other models, who were also raped. So I am really as guilty as they are. They raped me, but I went back for more, I was so mixed up. Rapist bondage photographers. I put them in touch with other models, who were abused as I was. Finally, enough was enough. I stopped answering their phone calls. They wrote to me, pleading for me to go back to them and do some more modeling. The phone rang and rang. I left the answering machine on. Every time I moved, it took them a year or so, but they found me. The phone would ring, and there they'd be. A nightmare come true! It didn't seem to matter that my numbers were never listed. They got my numbers anyway, somehow. They sent me gifts in the mail — t-shirts, recordings of songs they had written about me, old detective magazines — trying to bribe me to contact them and go back to work for them as their bondage model/victim. No way.

11. *A Wealthy Client*

I whipped Phil's ass, for a fee. Actually, Phil wasn't submissive, but he did have a switchable side. I heard he died about ten years ago. Rest in peace, Phil. Phil lived in Rockland County, and had been a professional ballroom dancer in his youth. He was the only heterosexual, wealthy retired ballroom dancer I have ever met. He acted in Hollywood movies and competed on the professional circuit. Apparently, he was very good, wisely saved his winnings, and well into his marriage, as he was getting too old to dance, he bought a shoe company specializing in shoes and costumes for young dancers. Tap shoes, toe shoes, character shoes. He did a lot of mail order, but mostly supplied shoes for dance schools for children. He showed me one of his catalogues, full of pictures of little girls posing proudly in tap outfits and Phil's dance shoes. Mommies' little jewels.

I knew Phil for quite a few years. Somehow, he knew The Professor, who made the introduction to me. Phil was loaded. He was still good friends with his ex-wife, an alcoholic, and paid the bills for the private plane she flew out in California. His mother was still alive, though legally blind, and rather than confine her to

a rest home and daylong radio, he kept her active, doing some sort
of simple piece work in the costume-making shop. He had a little
dog, a little poodle. Every time I went out to eat with Phil, he
insisted on a doggie bag — for a real doggie. He'd roll his eyes and
say, "I spoil that dog terribly, but she's my little baby." His little
baby regularly dined on filet mignon and new potatoes.

Phil used to meet me at The Professor's house. I think he
paid a tip to The Professor for the privilege — but I could be
wrong. At any rate, I was always assured a $200 fee from Phil, plus
$80 more, my standard fee from The Professor. After our joint
photography sessions, Phil would usually take us out to a nice
restaurant for all we could eat. I remember a Swiss meal once, with
rack of lamb. Phil's passion was spanking; or, rather, photos of
spanking. Like many of the perverts I've known over the years, he
shunned actual physical contact or any ongoing real relationship,
preferring instead to have custom photos taken. Then, he could
refer to them at his leisure, pleasuring himself with them privately. I had so many clients like Phil. I guess it is the ultimate in safe
sex. Because first of all, I usually didn't have sex with clients who
photographed me. I suppose I was willing enough, but it wasn't
even something most of them considered. They just wanted a
young female model who was a good sport.

In looking back on it all, I see my fees were very low, but a
lot of my clients were repeat customers — they had a kind of porn
addiction — and they simply were not going to stand for paying
more. I mean, I could have charged a high fee and worked for

them once, but I preferred to charge a lower fee and work for them on a repeat basis. One thing in common I had with my clients is that, unlike many females I have known, I, too, enjoy looking at erotic photographs and artwork. Most women I have known want security, cuddling, a real relationship — not sitting alone somewhere looking at dirty pictures and getting hot and bothered. Myself, I have a cold side to me, a skeptical, analytical side. I'd rather sit by myself all afternoon and read an erotic book than deal with going on a lunch date. What amazes me is that I have had as many love relationships as I have had. I am not just talking sexual relationships or encounters, I mean lovers — male lovers, at that. (I seem to be heterosexual. Sometimes I really think I'd rather be gay! I don't like men very much.)

I have had three husbands and two fiancés. Also, I have received more marriage proposals than any other female I know. Repeat: I don't much care for men. I don't think very highly of them. Go figure. My cold personality made me an asset for photographers like Phil. I could detach myself from what I was being posed to do — I knew it was a game. I didn't expect to build any meaningful relationships with the clients. I was just a kind of photographic hustler. But I also have a strong capability for empathy, so I was often able to guess accurately the mood and pose a client might want. I could usually judge which expression the client would want on my face. For example, would they want me to look fearful and submissive in a pose, or defiant, sort of sticking my tongue out at them, as if to say, "I dare you!?" For this reason, besides my reasonable fees and small requests for tips and extras, I had a lot of referral business.

I worked as a bondage model for about 20 years. I maintained a Post Office box. Many clients contacted me only through the mail. This seemed to suit a lot of them. They would select a time and place for meeting, and I would write back to their mail drop addresses and confirm or adjust the meeting time and place. As I was saying before, Phil liked photos of young girls being given corporal punishment — in the form of loving spankings. He would pose with a benevolent look on his face, as if to say, "There, there, naughty girl, you deserved that spanking, but I only did it for your benefit." I have many pictures of Phil pretending to comfort me after a severe spanking. In fact, he actually spanked me very, very few times. I remember most of the sessions being all for show, for the benefit of the camera. He was generous about sharing color prints, many of them large and clear and of the expensive type, with me and with The Professor.

Phil often posed as submissive, kissing my dressage boots, while I, clad in leather clothing and kid gloves, pretended to administer a small cat o'nine tails to his butt. He was interested in actually receiving a whipping from me once, and I obliged. He wanted to fully understand what the pain of being spanked or whipped was like. He was a very scientific kind of pervert. He, himself, was a good actor. He put a lot of feeling into pathetically and submissively clinging to my boot.

As I write these recollections, I find myself wondering about so many things. Is money our prime motivator? I would say it is not. I think I told myself at the time that I was posing for these pictures because I wanted a model's fee, and knew how to provide a specialty. But there was, of course, much more to it, and I was even aware of this at the time. People who model tend to be vain or have a streak of narcissism. Yet, sometimes, I think I was posing as I did as a kind of atonement, or self-punishment. Other times, I think I was doing it for sadistic reasons — "to punish those perverts — to make them pay for being weirdos" What I wasn't counting on was how emotionally involved I did get with some of these clients, such as The Professor, or Joe and Jane up in Vermont (although I basically didn't like them, I kept going back for more — a real love/hate thing going on). Joe and Jane were clearly abusing me (Joe was raping me orally), and yet, I went back for more abuse from them.

The Professor I loved because he was a very steady client, and gave me introductions, but also I loved him based on the merits of his fascinating personal history, sense of humor, and the tug-of-war I often had with him over small things, such as having an eclair for dessert or not. It sounds silly. I wish I were making all this up! I could not, and do not, recommend young people (or old) to get involved in the type of specialty modeling I was doing. I carved a niche for myself, and still sell old photos of myself through the mail from time to time. But certainly, this is not a "good" thing to do. It is, inherently, dishonorable.

Or is it? I mean, who is being harmed here? I guess it isn't a victimless crime. Did some of the family members of some of my clients find their stashes of photos of me and were they hurt by them? I believe in one case, this did happen. I had a client named Charles up on Cape Anne, Massachusetts, who had hired me a number of times, then gotten in a severe traffic accident. His head injuries were so extensive, he was not expected to live. In about the third month of his coma, his wife started looking through his files, to find, for instance, his life insurance policy. She found it — along with his stash of photos of young female models (myself and some other women). She divorced him and kept the child. He came out of his coma, and his brain damage eventually healed almost 99 per cent.

After not hearing from him for a few years, I did finally hear from him again, and learned the unfortunate facts about the effects of his photography fetish on his innocent family. But I continued to see him — in fact, more than ever. Although he was divorced, he had visitation rights with this his son regularly. He blamed himself for the divorce. He was very frank with me about it, and very calm. "It was my fault," he said simply. "My wife asked me to be faithful to her after we were married. I promised to. And then, I wasn't faithful. So I am wrong, and she was right to divorce me."

Phil liked me a lot. He said I was his type — full of life, loving good food and drink. He invited me to join him on a first-class pleasure cruise as his guest, all expenses paid, plus a little extra for me if I posed for him during the cruise. I suggested he take his ex-wife, instead, and he said he'd love to, but her alcoholism prevented her from travailing by sea, where there tended to be a lot of drinking on those fancy cruise ships. He pressed me to accompany him, and I would have loved to (to this day, I have never cruised) but I had already met the man who was to become my second husband, and was too in love to leave him for a week to go cruising with Phil.

I suggested Phil contact a straight (but sex-loving) girlfriend of mine, Natalie. He did, but their phone conversation turned sour when he suggested she wear a tight corset during some of the cruise. So I introduced him to Stripe, one of the phone girls at The Grand Central of Sleaze. She not only went on the cruise with him and enjoyed it, she posed for him (I saw the pictures, later) and cruised with him at least once more. She brought back gifts for me, paid for by Phil, of course: an evening bag, and a large bottle of Ivoire de Balmain perfume.

Stripe asked me about five years ago whatever happened to Phil, and I had to break the news to her that I that I had heard that he had passed away. I think she was very sad, upon hearing this. She got quiet and left the room for a few minutes. I think she was very attached to Phil, and not just for the money and good times he had given her. One thing remained important to Phil above all others, in connection with most of the photos for which he hired models to pose for him: his staged scenes of comforting the models (or himself being comforted, if he was on the receiving end of a slap on the butt) after the spanking. I believe Phil had a very tender side. In more ways than one!

12. *Posing For Myself*

I sift through my collections of photographs of myself and select one. I look at it. I see a dirty men's room somewhere, a dirty tiled floor. I see a urinal. I see a young woman in a lacy, see-through black top, a miniskirt, a motorcycle chain belt, and boots of some sort. I see her face is made up, she seems to have shaved her pubic hairs and has a tan line, and she wears a cross around her neck, and a rosary. I realize it's a photograph of myself, but looking at it feels so abstract.

I am not entirely sure who took the picture. I remember some guys, let's call them Connolly, a father and a son. I'll call them Connolly because I am not sure what their names really were, nor how I should go about contacting them. They gave me this photograph, so I assume I have permission to use it. I gave them permission to use it in any way they pleased, when they took it. They sold photos to men's magazines, they said. Maybe they sold pictures of me. I have no idea. I do know that whenever I visit a porn shop, I still see pictures of myself on magazine and book covers.

Of course, I've had some tricks recognize me. Probably employers and co-workers at straight jobs, and this may account somewhat for my rather checkered resumé (though I think not —

I usually quit jobs after two years because I was bored with them, or got fired for getting drunk, "having a bad attitude", etc.). You may very well be wondering how I got into this Bizarre Life. The answer is, in part: My real name is Lisa B. Falour. I think it is important for women in the sex industry to speak up and use their real family names. We have to blaze the trail. Not to glorify our actions, but to attempt to save families and children from exploitation, which often comes from the ignorance of the families about what their own children have done. Only by declaring ourselves publicly and risking complete rejection can we hope to make any progress. My own family will not acknowledge the sexual, disturbed aspect of myself, except to shun me, or to say nothing, or to make useless, contentless contacts, or, as my mother does, to mail me cryptic notes saying, "I was wrong. It's all my fault." Which is an adult way of saying, "Fuck you." It's how adult punks say fuck you to their kids.

Everyone knows that when there are family or personal problems, it's no longer a question of right and wrong — no black and white, only gray areas. Saying, "I was wrong," or "I am wrong" doesn't do any good. Not only is such a statement essentially nonsensical, it isn't constructive — it's probably counterproductive and destructive. What probably is right is for family members to say to one another, "I love you. I don't know what to do. I am so sorry you are hurting or that I made you hurt. Please tell me how to help you." But this just isn't what families seem to do. Or seem to want to do.

I never wanted to have a child. My childhood was a horror, and I never wanted to bring forth another life to suffer as I had. Finally, with my third marriage, I knew a man I could trust enough, and I wanted to have a child with him. But I was already in my late 30s, and we couldn't afford to have a child in the United States. In theory, I'd like to have a son or daughter. But I'm glad it didn't happen in my first marriage to Wolfe the Junkie, because I sensed that I was being pressured to produce an heir for his nouveau riche family. I was in my early 20s, and wanted most of all to finish my bachelor's degree. I didn't feel ready to get pregnant, so I was careful not to, not with Wolfe. My second marriage, which lasted for a total of 9 years legally and 2 years as lovers... well, I will try to tell you about that, because there may be something about it you may want to know. Another chapter. If I can. It's hard to write about. Very, very painful. I didn't want the children of Husband Two. I am not Jewish, and his family is, and being Jewish is so terribly important to them that I am sure the childrearing issue would have been a problem for us all. Of course I believe that if family members remain close and united, many basic family problems can be avoided. One of the worst deterrents to progress and to healing is silence. People should say, but do not say, "My daughter is a prostitute. How can I help her?" It would be good if more people could say, "My child is disturbed. I cannot cope. Help me."

Again, I look at myself in the photograph. I think it was taken late in 1981. I had already done a lot of posing, and wasn't completely satisfied with what I had seen the photographers I'd worked with produce. I like models to look real — I look closely at the picture and see a bruise on my raised arm. Something for the airbrushes of the fancier men's magazines to deal with. But that was the reality of the pose — I had a bruise — and I like it that the bruise shows. No airbrushing. Best of all, I like it when the model has had a hand in setting up the shot and the pose — when he or she participated in the production of the product. I requested and arranged for this photograph to be taken. I did my own makeup, wore my own clothes.

Men's rooms excite me. Urinals, urine, the act of male urination fascinates me. Like many women, I am sexually excited at the smell of urine. I enjoy "water sports" I wanted to produce a sexy, interesting photo which was also a portrait of the model's — that is to say, my — personality. I did that. The Connollys developed and printed the photos and gave me a few of them, along with the understanding they would then be free to sell them. But as I've said before, I don't know if they ever did sell them or not.

I cannot bring myself to feel ashamed about all the sexy posing I've done over the years. I find myself remembering enjoying the work too much (usually), and most of all, enjoying the finished photos. I have a huge collection of photos of myself. I look at them from time to time and feel a combination of pride and shame. I feel confused by them, but mostly because I feel more pride than I do shame. I had a strong feeling that before long, I'd be fat and forty. And here I am — just that. I'd look in a mirror and see a young face, and find myself seeing the skull beneath that young face. My hair is beginning to gray, I'm finally starting to get lines around my eyes. I'm overweight, out of shape. I've never feared aging or death. Such things did not motivate me to pose. I wanted a record of how I looked in my youth. I knew it would be over quickly — my youthful looks — and it was.

13. *Pimp*

Another photo. M. Henry Jones (he doesn't like to use his first name) poses with me on our East Ninth Street New York rooftop, possibly in early 1981. We were crazy in love. He always grabbed me and played a little rough, which I liked.

I dropped out of Kent State University in Ohio and moved to the New York area on Hallowe'en, 1977. I had answered an ad in a newspaper for a "mother's helper", and was hired to live with a couple of doctors and their three children in Westchester County, New York, clean their house every day, and watch their three kids. Over the winter I visited my old college chum, Miriam Linna, who had moved to New York to be the first drummer for The Cramps (instead of going on to get her Master's degree under a scholarship at The University of Helsinki, Finland).

Miriam was better than a cool big sister to me — so I was always tagging along after her on my days off. I'd ride the Metro North train down to Grand Central, hop onto the 6 train, and run down to the East Village to run wild with Miriam. We went out a lot together to hear live music, and she introduced me to a group called The Fleshtones. They were New York City art school punks who could barely play their instruments, yet wrote their own material and put on fantastic live performances. The audiences were whipped up into dance frenzies! The Fleshtones were wonderful. They liked '60s music and r'n'b, covered Screamin' Jay Hawkins besides, did short sets and lots of instrumentals, and when they played their own stuff, they sang of their late '70s New York City angst.

Miriam was friendly with them, and introduced me. I took one look at their lead singer, Peter Zaremba, fell in love, went back to Ohio, packed a suitcase, and moved to Manhattan to be near him. I had about $40 cash and about $300 in a check I'd written payable to myself, which, once deposited, took two long weeks to clear, since it was from out of State. (I was too young to understand banking laws.) In my haste, I'd forgotten to pack basics such as my glasses. I am nearsighted, and wandered around my new home squinting at street signs, trying to figure out where the hell I was.

New Yorkers will either kill you or give you the shirts off their backs — in my case, many were very kind to me, and approached me and asked me if I was lost. When I replied I was and was new in town, they gave me directions, warning me about blocks to avoid on my way. (The late '70s in New York were very, very rough.) I called Peter from Ohio. He was seldom at his mother's house in Queens, so I dialed Miriam's number, hoping to find him there. "No, Lisa, he's not here," she said, and my heart fell. "Wait a minute!" she commanded. "I hear something. Hang on!" She threw down the phone, and I held my breath. She came back on line: "It's Zaremba and some 'Tones! They're coming up the stairs. Hang on a minute!" (She lived on the top floor of an East Fifth Street tenement, and it took a long time to climb her stairs.)

"Hullo?" Zaremba was on the line. I wanted to leap through the wires to be with him! I'd had a few dates in my last six months of high school, but had never really had "a boyfriend." In fact, because I was date-raped when I was 17, I hung out with lesbians at Kent State and declared myself a man-hater. All that changed when I beheld Zaremba. He was a walking disaster. He was my dream come true. He went to art school (where he was failing), chewed his nails, popped pep pills, had bad skin, and a sweet and sleepy smile that would absolutely melt me. I didn't love him so much as he was worshiped. "Peter? It's Lisa. I miss you. I'm coming back to New York."

"Great!" he said.

"Why don't I meet you after rehearsal at Phoebe's tonight? Say, around ten?"

He sounded truly surprised, but very, very happy. "Okay," he said.

I can still hear his voice. The Queens accent. He hung up the phone and I ran downstairs to ask my mother to drive me to the airport in Cleveland, Ohio immediately. I don't know what my parents thought about my dropping out of art school after only two years of a four-year program, but my mother was very sure she didn't want me to run off to New York. "You'll wind up a bum," were her exact words. I shook with rage, wept, and wrote her a long letter in my old bedroom, telling her I was off to follow my dreams and make something of my life. When she left me at the entrance gate to the waiting airplane, I was too excited to pause for more than a moment to thank her for the ride and to kiss her goodbye. I was never close to my parents — we weren't a kissy bunch. "Bye!" I said breathlessly, and pulled away from Mom.

"Goodbye," she said quietly. "I hope you find your heart's desire."

I turned my back on her and walked confidently down the ramp, stopping to turn only once to wave and smile. I was sure I was going to. I supposed eventually I did. I suppose also her admonition about my becoming "a bum" came true, but I finished art school and got a Bachelor's degree, married and divorced a millionaire (Wolfe), worked in Wall Street, got a Master's degree, and later married a writer I helped build into a successful paperback writer, so, except for the one half of my life which has almost always been decidedly sleazy, I proved Mom wrong. Mothers usually know, but in this case, my Mom only saw half my future.

I got off the plane at La Guardia Airport and realized I hadn't thought about a place to stay. I went to a payphone and made some calls. Finally, I located a photographer named Fran who was a friend of a friend. I asked her if I could park my suitcase in her 12th Street apartment while I looked for a place to stay. "Um, I have to go out in 20 minutes," she said.

"I'll be right there! Please wait for me!" I begged. By the time I got to East 12th Street, Fran was gone.

I lugged my suitcase up five flights of stairs and sat in her hallway, panting, disgusted with myself for already losing my umbrella — I'd left it hanging on the payphone in the airport. I calmed down after a few minutes, and lugged the suitcase (bright red plastic — what a sight I must have been!) to St. Marks Place, where the bass player for the Fleshtones shared an apartment with his sister, Lisa, and a nudist hippie whose name I've forgotten.

Marek, the bass player, lived on the top floor of a seven-story building. I rang the buzzer, was relieved to get an answer, and lugged the suitcase up the narrow seven flights. The hippie opened the door. He was nude, of course! He recognized me right away. I'd been there before. "Hi, Lisa! C'mon in! What's happening?"

"Hi, I've just moved to Manhattan! Can I leave my suitcase here tonight? I'm on my way to meet Zaremba."

"No prob!" he chirped. I tried not to stare at his penis. He was very tall and his long blonde hair fell down his back.

"Um, could I sleep here tonight on the floor?" I ventured.

"Yeah, sure," he replied, "but make sure Marek pulls down the foam pad for you. He's lazy. Don't sleep directly on the floor. What time will you be here?" I was swimming in oceans of relief.

"Probably not til morning. I'll probably be out all night with Zaremba."

"Okay, cool," the hippie said, "but I can't give you any keys — we don't have a spare set. So when you get here, I may or may not be in, dig?"

"Oh, sure," I said happily, called my parents in Ohio and left the phone number and told them I'd safely arrived, and ran off to Phoebe's to meet Zaremba.

It was about 7:30 p.m. I was hungry, but didn't really feel I could spare the money to eat anything. Still, I couldn't very well sit at a table by the window at Phoebe's on the Bowery and watch for Zaremba to walk by after rehearsal without ordering anything. Fuck it, I decided. I was so excited, so positive about everything, I decided it might be my last night on Earth, but I'd spend it with Zaremba, and damned if I wasn't going to have something in my stomach before I met my Maker. I ordered a slice of quiche, which came with a small free salad, and a single glass of wine. I inhaled it, watching out the window anxiously for Zaremba and his fellow Fleshtones to walk North on the East side of Bowery from the rehearsal space they shared with The Cramps in the basement of a building owned by Andy Warhol, who'd been wisely snapping up downtown real estate.

Right at eight, just as we'd arranged, they walked by. I tapped on the glass, smiling and waving at Zaremba. His eyes met mine and he and rushed in to hug me, followed by his fellow band members. He enfolded me in a bear grip, lifting me slightly off my feet. "You came! I can't believe it!" he gushed. I squeezed him and pulled away to say a breathless hello to the other 'Tones, who were standing there awkwardly, but who seemed very pleased to see me again.

"Hi, guys!" I shouted.

"Hi, Lisa!" they replied.

"Well, what now?" I said to Zaremba. He was nearly beside himself with joy.

"First order of the evening is beer," he said in an official-sounding, deep voice. The guys cheered. Off we went to the nearest bodega to buy some quarts of Miller beer, which were 65 cents each at the time.

We all went up to Marek's place with the nude hippie, to drink and plan our evening. I was flying on air. It was a mild night in late March 1978. I held Peter's arm tight, feeling that everything was going my way, and would always. I threw my head back and looked up at the sky. Despite the city lights, the stars were bright, the sky was wild, open and crazy, and I was in love, where I wanted to be, and on my Big Adventure.

New York in the late '70s! Urban decay in its extreme form. Someone should have sealed off an entire city block back then, and put it in a museum for future generations to ponder. The city was as good as broke, and public services had been cut to a minimum. A few police stayed in their cruisers, not getting out for much of anything, there was a reduced force of firefighters, and only sporadic trash collection. Dog shit everywhere! (The laws hadn't been changed yet.) Even in the cool weather, the smell was strong — the smell of things falling apart. My adrenaline was gushing. If this wasn't a challenge, what was? Could I make it here? Would I survive? I didn't know, didn't care. I was determined to go out with a bang.

Studio 54 was a good place to start. Everyone called it "Studio." We went with a small-time drug dealer whose claim to fame was that he could always get himself and his friends into

Studio for free. We swallowed strong amphetamines, drank gin and tonics (who needs a liver?), and while the artificial snow fell, Zaremba kissed me while we lounged on a dirty couch in the back of that cavernous disco. On the way downtown in the cab at dawn he kissed me again, our teeth smashing into one another's as the Checker hit yet another pothole. As the driver cursed us for failing to tip, I said goodbye to Zaremba, who was apologetic that he had to get back to Queens for a dental appointment. He'd lost one of his crowns while biting the aforementioned small-time drug dealer on the leg during a previous foray into the world of Studio, and the tooth had fallen into the artificial snow and been lost forever. I didn't think (never have, in fact) to ask exactly why anyone would bite someone else's leg in a public discotheque, but bizarre behavior was definitely the norm in the New York I first knew.

I climbed the steps, and the nude hippie, now disheveled and roused from his sleep, let me in and I tried to sleep on a piece of foam rubber, but the sun was coming up and I was on speed. I went into the tiny bathroom and washed up a little. This was no time for lollygagging. Had to find a place to stay and a job and only had about $38 in cash left to my name.

I found a "room", which was actually just a partitioned section in a big loft at 111 East 14th Street, for $35 a week. The place belonged to a sweet, alcoholic black guy who got heart attacks in his spare time, and worked doing data entry at Citibank in between Welfare checks The three little "rooms" in the back had been formerly occupied by Nico and by Patty Hearst during her spell of hiding in New York, he claimed. Though it wasn't really legal for him to discriminate, he preferred to rent only to young white single females.

One of them was named Jackie. She was on Welfare, was about to become an unwed mother, and read and reread a used paperback book about baby care. Her boyfriend called from time to time, drunk. My other co-renter was from "Upstate" (that's all she'd say, that was as specific as she would be) and spoke shockingly fluent Chinese (I don't know which dialect) and worked as the receptionist for a Chinese dentist in Chinatown.

The place was dark and buggy. The sweet black alcoholic guy had a goldfish bowl with some kind of parasite in it, and a big swimming pool, which I was actually drunk enough to swim in one night when I came home alone very late. The bottom of that pool, an aboveground suburban model, was all slimy. It was covered by a big tent. Right in the loft — just like at the circus or a fancy outdoor wedding. I found out later the pool broke the ceiling beams and flooded the building, which was torn down soon after.

Some genuine gypsies (first I'd ever met) lived on the floor below us, and advertised for a five dollar palm reading which cost way more than five dollars, natch. When I asked one of their children one day why he wasn't in school, he just grinned and shook his head. Luchow's was across the street, though respectable people seldom ventured into that neighborhood just East of Union Square anymore. Downstairs, among the old S. Klein buildings complex (torn down during the mid80s), was an Everyone's Discount Store,

Massaab Brothers Pawn Brokers, and a Hispanic lunch counter
with six stools. There, I bought my breakfast each morning for the
next four months (until I put a slice of bread into the toaster,
turned it on, and a mouse jumped out — then, I moved to East
10th Street) for only 65 cents.

The tired man behind the counter sweated profusely and
smiled kindly at me as I counted out sixty five pennies and hungrily ate everything placed before me each morning. The breakfast
was Spanish coffee (the grounds are boiled right along with the
milk) in a paper cup, a very small orange juice, toasted bread,
french fries, and two eggs. Across the way was a place called the
Central Soda Lunch, which was open 24 hours. When I'd get
insomnia, pining for Zaremba and listening to the mice scratch, I'd
go down there at 3:00 a.m., spend a dollar, and get pancakes, juice,
coffee and greasy sausage. I had my first egg cream at the Central.
I've always liked to eat, and New York is very much about food.
When I think about what I miss most about New York (I live in
Europe now), it's mostly food items, such as White Castle burgers
bought in downtown Brooklyn and eaten on the Esplanade.

I went to the Strand Bookstore and applied for a job.
Miriam worked there, at Patti Smith's former desk. They seemed
willing to hire me, but on a hunch, I took the train uptown and
visited my favorite store in New York: the Paradise Bootery, just
above Times Square. Anyone with a shoe fetish who's been to New
York in the not-so-distant past remembers this place fondly. Run
by an old concentration camp survivor named Alex, it was heaped

with dusty racks of shoes and boots that were dreams come true for hookers of every stripe. I used to browse in there often, sometimes picking up a size 3_ (!) spike-heeled, leopard print mule and stroking it when I thought no one was looking. I asked the old man for a job there, and he looked at me strangely and was silent for a long time. Then, he directed me to visit his wife, who worked in a very upscale shoe and handbag boutique near Bloomie's, and had one worker out on vacation. "No promises after my employee comes back in two weeks," she told me. I said fine, and started working there the next day.

My basic salary was about $100 a week after taxes, but I could earn 2 per cent commission on every pair of shoes I sold. It was sink or swim — I learned to dress up, put on makeup, and talk to people, convincing them any way I could they had to have the damned shoes, no matter how silly they looked in them. I had been painfully shy and withdrawn before. In this pond, the ugly duckling had to learn to squawk. This very kind woman kept me employed for my first year of living in Manhattan. I was thrilled to meet and speak to shoe browsers such as actresses Diane Keaton and Carol Lynley, but far more intrigued by our more eccentric clients.

A lady who called herself "Jessica" had a size four foot — incredibly tiny — and left her phone number with my boss, Alex's wife, who was named Ibolya and was Hungarian. "She's a Rothschild, I theeenk," Ibolya said to me one day about Jessica. Another interesting customer was known to us as Nora. She'd often meet her jeweler boyfriend at Gino, a chic bar next door, but would come to visit us and shop and have her coffee right there in the showroom (she pulled it out of a little paper deli bag) and moan about her lonely life. "Do you know who Louis B. Mayer was?" she asked me.

"Of course," I replied. "Hollywood."

"I am his daughter," she replied with a very, very weird smile.

While I was learning to spiel in the shoe store, Zaremba dumped me and went off to deflower other females, but not before introducing me to M. Henry Jones. Henry went to the same art school as Zaremba, and was making a short animated film called "Soul City", which consisted of The Fleshtones playing a song by that name. I became friendly with Henry, and we began dating. By the end of the Summer of 1978, we started having sex. He was your basic, all-American hallucinating schizophrenic speed freak filmmaker from your basic psychotic North American late 1970s punk scene. I wouldn't say it was love at first sight, but the way he yanked me upside down by the ankles one day and suspended me in front of him while he ate my pussy does remain in my memory. He was incredibly strong.

We had an arrangement: Since I was tortured by nightmares, especially since I'd taken Cortisone for years for arthritis as a kid, it was agreed that I'd sleep on Henry's self-constructed loft bed in his East 9th Street apartment while he worked on his animated films on his bathtub lid all night. (This is called a cold-water flat. Many East Village apartments still have the bathtub in the kitchen, or main room. It's covered with a metal lid, usually.)

Further, it was agreed that each time I'd cry out, he'd come and wake me up and comfort me, then go back to his animation work on his bathtub lid. It was a nice arrangement, and I got the first good sleep I'd had in years.

He never pressured me to have sex with him. Very decent guy. When we did have sex, it was by mutual agreement. During all this time, I got very interested in his work. He had been a child prodigy, and was in art school on a scholarship. He could, it seemed to me, do anything with a camera. Just give him time, chocolate donuts and lots of coffee, and he could pretty much manage any type of photography, film-making or animation you'd need. Of course, strong amphetamines were on his menu. If you had them to offer him along with work and a little cash, this was the best guy in the world for your project (though he couldn't for the life of him meet deadlines).

He later went on to form his own studio and did amazing work in many media. He was the first person I ever knew who had a laser set up in his place so he could do holograms. In the 1970s! Henry turned me on to a new world of possibilities, and sexually, we turned each other on to a lot of odd stuff. For my honors program when I finally finished art school I made a 16mm film which was "a self-portrait in bondage", and Henry helped me arrange this. Another chapter will deal with this event. As a former Eagle Scout, he could tie some mean knots!

As 1978 wore on and my personal life took new turns, we fell in love and were known as a couple. By this point, I had moved into a shared apartment on East 10th Street, by the Russian baths, with a guy named Paul Martin, who was among those who helped me do my punk 'zine, BIKINI GIRL. The day after he graduated from art school, Henry had a complete nervous breakdown. He spent nearly four months in a famous mental hospital in New York. To say I was devastated would be a gross understatement. I was lost without him. He was over-medicated and given a long series of shock treatments. When he came out of the hospital, he had near-total amnesia. It seemed he'd have to give up his cheap apartment and move back Upstate with his family, because he couldn't even remember how to cook for himself. He needed a lot of care and retraining about how to live everyday life. (He didn't know which subway station to get off at, for example, to get home to his apartment.)

I moved out of Paul Martin's place and into Henry's place on East 9th Street. Every morning I'd serve him breakfast in bed with his Lithium — he was too weak and sick to his stomach from the pills to get up right away. The part-time secretarial job he'd found me in the Film Program of The American Federation of Arts paid only five dollars an hour, I had art school bills to pay, and I knew we needed money, so I stepped up my bondage modeling activities to get money for us to eat. Henry went to an outpatient hospital each day for almost a year, but when he wasn't there, he needed constant attention. An ethical problem arose: I knew Henry better than he knew himself, therefore could "build a man to order" That is, I could put him back together in such a way as to suit myself. He trusted me completely; he had to, really.

Since during his hospital stay I'd sought comfort in the arms of our mutual friend Brian, I taught him to look the other way with regard to my dalliances. I fed him his dinner each night, watched while he took a bath and brushed his teeth, tucked him in, kissed him, and went off to fuck Brian. I'd come back at dawn and make Henry his breakfast. I "trained" Henry to accept this as perfectly normal, whereas he certainly wouldn't have thought so before.

In late 1980 and throughout most of 1981, after my very brief departure from both Henry and Brian to marry and then walk out on Wolfe, my first husband, I worked as a call girl as well as a bondage model, to support myself and Henry. Every day I stuck a $20 bill on the refrigerator with a magnet so he'd have lunch and pocket money for himself. I made sure our bills were paid and that we always had something to eat. By this time he was not only lovesick and so naturally rather blind, I had trained him not to ask where it was I disappeared to for hours at a time several days a week, nor about the money that was suddenly in my wallet when I'd left the house broke just earlier that same day. And so in this way, Henry — unwittingly — became my first pimp. What I mean by this is, I was definitely "a working girl" by this point, and he took money from me. Technically, that makes a man a pimp — taking money from a whore. But he didn't know. At least, I don't think he knew. It's never been something we've discussed. Sad, huh? Sad for me, sad for him.

Over the years, I've known many prostitutes in similar situ-

I WAS FOR SALE.

ations: they do that work to support not a drug or an alcohol habit, but to put meals in front of their loved ones. Prostitution is definitely not, in my mind, a victimless crime. I did what I could to get outside help, such as food stamps, but didn't qualify for much assistance, and neither his family nor mine were very forthcoming (nor were they especially able!) with assistance. I felt that for us, as a couple, to go on Public Assistance was morally wrong — even more wrong than being paid for getting tied up and having my picture taken. That is because I was able-bodied, attending college, and working part time as a secretary.

Believe it or not, the $400 or so a month I earned from my straight job put us out of the running for quite a bit of Public Assistance. New York City was itself struggling financially, so as much as I reached out for help, I was told there was no help to be had. I went about the prostitution as cheerfully as I could; in fact, I usually enjoyed it (a mild pot habit helped ease the rough edges). When I look back on the situation we (Henry and myself) were in, I think I did just about the best I could to cope with things. Still... it's all terribly unfortunate, isn't it?

)164(

14. *Angelo*

Angelo took a photo of me in Henry's apartment sometime in 1979. His talent as an amateur photographer was already showing. I love the picture. Cropped just perfectly: just the bottom of a fancy bra showing, a ribbon which wasn't for show but which actually worked to squeeze the breasts slightly and add cleavage, hangs down over a young and supple flat belly. The navel is concealed. The underpants have such a long touch of frill, they look like a short slip. The garter belt is built for speed.

The stockings were from Phil's Hosiery in the East Village. Phil had a place on the West Side of First Avenue, between 9th and 10th Streets. I was terribly upset when he retired and died shortly thereafter. Even before I lived in New York, I made visits to Phil's. He had all the old-fashioned stuff you just can't find anymore in the U.S. (or any other place I know) at any price. Shear seamed stockings, the kind you needed a garter belt to wear. The heels of the stockings were decorated with a fancy pattern, running up the back of the calf. I love stockings. To this day, I don't believe I've ever worn real silk stockings.

A man wrote to me several times at my Post Office box and offered to buy me a real pair if he could fondle my legs in the backs of taxi cabs. His letters were lovely and he kept mentioning to me he was a friend of Emile de Antonio (did I spell that correctly?), but I never met with him because even though I knew real silk stockings were very expensive, I didn't think a pair of them, which would surely last only one night and be a pricey thrill, was fair trade for my "personal services" I mean, I don't think I was a greedy girl, but I at least wanted some cash on the side, maybe even a steak dinner. In some things, I held very firm. It does strike me as funny how many times I sold myself so cheap. I tried to be consistent, but life just doesn't always go that way.

I look again at the photograph. The gloves I am wearing in this photograph are of a synthetic material, and the silver bracelet was given to me as a gift when I was around ten years old, by my father. I wore it until I took it off one night in the loft of La Marquise, and foolishly forgot it there in her front room desk drawer until the next day. I went back and it was gone.

When I was about ten, my parents took a very unusual weekend off. My mother's mother came to babysit for my brother and I. My parents told us they were going to Williamsburg, and brought back wonderful gifts. I remember my brother got a compass of good quality, and a nasty soft plastic tiny replica of a shrunken head on a bouncy string of elastic, which we both adored. I think I got another gift besides the later-lost bracelet, but don't recall.

In 1986, when my mother was dying of cirrhosis of the liver (she subsequently recovered, to the astonishment of her doctors) she confessed to me she'd had an abortion around that time, because she and my father decided they just couldn't afford a third child. She's Catholic, so it was a big deal to her. Well, abortion is a big deal to most women. (I've had one. I know.) She fairly begged me to assure her that I wasn't angry with her for denying me another brother or a sister. I told her I was proud of her decision. I certainly still am. Unwanted pregnancy is a big deal. I confess, I used to sort of look down my nose at female friends who had frequent abortions or who had a child or two more than what they'd wanted, but after I got pregnant by accident in 1994, it hit me smack in the face how wrong I had been in my smugness.

I took a film-making class in art school in New York around 1979, and made a short, silent Super-8mm black-and-white film (which I dumped in a bucket of dye and tinted pink, my favorite color) I called "Girl Pack" While I was filming part of it on the sidewalk of East 10th Street, a young man came up to me and asked if he could take some pictures of my six punk actresses. I told him to go away. That was no ordinary young man. That was Angelo.

Angelo was born and raised on Christopher Street. He was a very bright kid and went to a high school for very good students. His father worked as a baker at the Biltmore Hotel (later at The Plaza, when the Biltmore closed), and his mother was just plain ol' nutty. By the time I met him, he had some serious self-esteem problems (maybe it was all those times the Puerto Rican kids mugged him at school, I dunno), and had ceased bathing on any regular basis. His bugeyes fixed me, his face was impassive, he spoke in an articulate monotone. He worked in the philosophy paperbacks section of Barnes & Noble, went to photography school, and every Sunday, worked in a store in the West Village called Exotic Aquatics, mostly as a means to buy strange creatures for pets at a discount.

He had a pair of Madagascar hissing cockroaches, a Tegu lizard, a Burmese python, an alligator snapping turtle, various fish, a soft-shelled turtle, striped mud turtles, and many things he called "terrariums", but which looked more to me like ordinary jars of slime. He was an avid porn consumer. He was also a 'zine reader, and had previously written to me in connection with mine: BIKI-NI GIRL. He'd asked me if I could introduce him to any women who could tie him up. I wrote back and said no, but that I approved of his proclivities. I enclosed my personal card (pink, of course) with my unlisted telephone number on it, and of course, he called. He asked if he could become my slave. At that point in my life, I hadn't yet fully embarked on my voyage in the world of S/M, so his suggestion shocked me. "No!" I said firmly.

"Think about it," he pressed on. "Having a slave could make your life much easier."

"How?" I asked. I remember I was kind of horrified at the very concept. (Don't tell any of my current slaves, please!)

"Well, I can do stuff for you. Housework and stuff."

"I do my own housework!" I retorted. "I don't need a slave!"

"Okay," he said calmly, "but think about it. I could do your laundry or something. It would be a privilege."

I didn't say yes right at that moment, but I did say yes very shortly thereafter. He knocked on my door at the appointed time, I opened the door and handed him my dirty laundry wrapped up in my dirty bedsheet, he thanked me, and bounced off. Two hours later, he came back, the laundry clean, dry and folded — and he'd pay for it. Good deal, I thought! This went on for quite a long time. Eventually, I started inviting him in for coffee or a joint, and chatting with him. He interested me. He always had something cool to show me, or something very funny to say, or sometimes, a small gift. He was very thoughtful and thrifty — he often found great stuff in flea markets and such. My roommate, Paul Martin, was slightly bemused by my "slave", but couldn't say anything against it, as we weren't lovers, and Angelo came and went punctually and reliably, and even washed the dishclothes we both used, as well as Paul's soiled bath towels. He just kind of shook his head and smiled and said, "Cool, Lisa! Go fer it!" (One of his pet sayings was "go fer it." He was the first person I ever heard use it.)

15. *Lisa In Bondage*

Back in the late '70s and early '80s, I didn't see anyone doing pure bondage films; that is, film or video, which showed only a woman (or man) completely tied up, struggling to get free. These days, that type of product is available, but back then, it wasn't. I wanted to be the first to do a pure bondage film. The strange couple in Vermont had given me a couple of short reels of brittle movie footage they'd found at a flea market somewhere. They were old Irving Klaw stag films, and had titles like, "Juliette Learns the Ropes, Part II." I enjoyed looking at them, but they had no sound, and the movements of the models seemed jerky and unspontaneous. I did like seeing the old-time lingerie and hair and makeup styles, and the way the models tiptoed around on their high, high heels. I wanted to do a modern version of such a film, but with sound. Naturally, I wanted to be the star.

It was not long after I'd left Wolfe, my first husband (whom I'd met at The Hellfire Club and married a week later, only to find out later he was into heroin), so this would place things around January, 1981. I was on Christmas break — most of the schools in town were closed for the holidays. I hung around The School of

Visual Arts on 23rd Street so much (Angelo, Brian, Peter, Henry and other people I knew went to school there), the security guards thought I attended, and always let me in. Henry had an arrangement with one of the security guards who worked night shift to let him in at all hours to work on his animated films. Without the knowledge or the permission of the art school, we commandeered one of the empty rooms one night, unrolled the backdrop paper, set up lights, and prepared to make my movie. It was to be a "self-portrait in bondage", and I had vague ideas of presenting it to my own art school (Hunter College) and asking for credit for it as part of my honors thesis.

Finally, I chickened out. I never showed the film to any of my teachers or advisors. I ended up having so many credits (I'd attended five different undergraduate schools by the time I qualified for an undergraduate degree) I was allowed to select a Bachelor of Science rather than a Bachelor of Arts degree, anyway. I'd drifted off into Eastern philosophy and Early Christian Art classes, dabbled in Beat Literature forums, and just generally didn't know what the hell I was doing in school anymore. You know how it is.

I went to 14th Street to shop for my lingerie. I got a white strapless bra, a white corselette with attached panties (and snap-fastened crotch), a white garter belt, white stockings, and little white silky ankle socks. My high, high red patent leather heels finished the outfit. I bought most of the stuff at a big shop with bins of clothes, that catered to Hispanic brides-to-be. "You getting married?" the cashier asked me.

"Um, yes," I answered. (What could I tell her? No, this is for my bondage movie?)

"Good luck," she smiled, handing me my bag and receipt. I'll need it, I thought, as I hurried out of that place. I'll never understand what compels me to do strange projects like this one. I mean, what was the point? I didn't really know then, and I definitely don't know now. I just felt I had to do it. To express myself in this bizarre way. Go figure.

I went to the ladies' toilet and put on my makeup, while Henry directed a small volunteer crew to get ready for the shoot. We were prepared to be caught and thrown out of the building at any point. I'd bought two reels of 16mm black-and-white movie film, with sound, and we had a camera from somewhere (possibly the school's film department — I don't remember). I don't recall who the crew were, except one of them was a very gifted film and photography student named Barry. His parents lived out on Staten Island in an old house that was attached to a (non-working) windmill. This area of Staten Island is called Tottenville, and was so rural, many of the roads were unpaved, and lots of people kept a horse or two on their property. Barry was short of funds but extremely intrepid — since he didn't have the money to develop any of his 16mm films, he trained himself how to develop them, in a garbage can filled with chemicals in the family garage. His finished home-developed movies had a unique, gray and grainy quality. He was the only person who got "paid" for working on the shoot, and all he got was a reel of unused film. The others — I don't remember who or how many they were — got nothing except sandwiches and hot coffee.

It was a very cold winter, and since it was vacation time, the school had shut down its central heating system. It was cold! The poured concrete floor felt like ice (except ice is perhaps more yielding). Once I was dressed, Henry put his Eagle Scout experience to good work and tied me up expertly, using neat, tight knots. I put a plastic practice golf ball in my mouth. It was strung through with a piece of cord. I pushed it in as far as it would go, and Henry tied the cord behind my head as tightly as he could. Within a few minutes, the skin around my lips was irritated and began to bleed. Bloody saliva dripped from my mouth during the shoot, but since the film is in black-and-white, you can't tell I was bleeding. But I was. My elbows were pulled behind my back and bound, then cinched so tightly, my elbows were close together. (But not nearly touching, the way Bettie Page was able to do it. She must have been made of rubber!) My legs were bent at the knee, and the thighs and calves were bound together, then cinched. Henry took some strong medical adhesive tape and pulled it around and around my hands, until they were in a sort of tape mitten. My ankles were tied together and cinched. A rope ran between my hands and my ankles — I was "hogtied."

I get no pleasure out of being bound; in fact, I am claustrophobic and hate to be restricted in any way. I don't even like wearing tight clothes or footwear. This fear of being caught and held in one place runs very deep. I think it goes back to the womb. I think that as I was trapped inside my mother's body, while she smoked and drank and took pills of various types, I wanted OUT. Instead of feeling protected, I believe I felt horror. (I also have fears about heights and water, so forced myself to go on an Outward Bound-type program in 1977, canoeing and rock climbing in Canada. After about five days of fear like ice water running through my veins, I relaxed, and the fears subsided somewhat.) I think I experimented with bondage games because being tied up scares me so badly. I think it was a way of testing my limits. Then again, maybe I am just fucking nuts. I've never understood how anyone can calmly submit to being bound, lie still and accept it without a struggle. A gut-churning terror comes over me. I begin to panic almost at once.

When we made this movie, I cheated a little and took half a Valium just before I was tied. Once I was tied, Henry carried me out to the center of the seamless paper, where we had set the stage, and everyone stepped back, adjusting their lights. Since the film was shot with sound, the volunteer crew had to be very quiet. I'd told Henry to wait until I started freaking out, then to start filming me. I didn't last long before I gave him the sign with a frantic toss of my head. Barry was behind the camera and started filming. My pain was very real at this point and I struggled to find a comfortable position. No such thing existed, especially not on a freezing cold poured concrete floor. Added to all this was my fear the security guard would pop in any time and bust us. We had all agreed to do only one shot, Warhol-style, until the roll of film was used up — about 10 minutes. To say it was the longest ten minutes of my life would be trite, but pretty accurate. At one point, one of my shoes slipped off. I struggled to get it back on. My moans on the soundtrack are not so much cries of pain and pleas to be untied as they are sighs and squeals of frustration. I am so vain, I just did not want my self-portrait in bondage to be spoiled by having me wearing only one shoe throughout! It was the middle of the night. I could hear light traffic going by outside on 23rd Street. My personal life was a mess, I'd walked out on my new rich husband, I was working as a call-girl and in a straight whorehouse to survive and pay my college bills, and I was lying on the floor in an infinity of pain. People who've seen this movie have said it's torture in itself to watch it. You have to be very, very sadistic to enjoy all ten minutes of "Lisa in Bondage."

When the film ran out, Barry said, "Cut," quietly. Henry hurried over and began to slice away the cords he couldn't untie. I had fought so hard, the knots had tightened. As soon as I was free, I hobbled to a chair, massaging myself to get the blood flowing again. The ropes had left bright red impressions in my flesh. The marks took weeks to disappear completely. I don't know exactly what kind of statement I was trying to make with this movie, but it's a statement of something or other, that's for sure. Maybe a statement about my own suffering, the suffering of humanity and the planet, the futility of struggle — I didn't know then, and I don't know now. The best I can come up with is that it's "a self-portrait in bondage."

As soon as I could, I changed into street clothes and helped the crew restore the room to its former state. No evidence could remain of our unauthorized visit or heads would roll somewhere at The School of Visual Arts, and I didn't want that. To my present shame, I hesitated to give Barry the unused roll of film. I was tired, and kept thinking about how much it had cost me. "C'mon, Lisa, give it him!" Henry whispered. I handed it to Barry, and he grinned. It's so hard to be generous and thoughtful when you've just been through 15 or 20 minutes of bondage under bright lights, along with the constant fear of being caught and getting in trouble. Of course, I should have tipped the rest of the crew with cash, but I don't think I did. Everyone worked for free.

Henry never played bondage games with me, didn't approve of the project, but couldn't bring himself to point an accusing finger at me. The project was an artistic one, and he realized I had every right to express myself in the way I chose. Henry played rough role-playing-type games with me, but tying me up wasn't quite his bag. He was pretty quiet about my "self-portrait in bondage." "Henry did the knots," I'd announce to people I showed the finished film to, and he'd squirm if he was there. When it came time to do the soundtrack, I had an idea. While I am in bondage, everything distorts: time; pain levels; emotions; sound. The first three I couldn't control artistically, but the last one — sound — I could. Henry got me an appointment at a fancy sound recording studio in midtown Manhattan. (I have long ago forgotten its name. I have also forgotten what I paid for the sound work, but it was a lot.) A professional sound recording technician stood at the ready and manipulated a large control panel to achieve the effects I requested. I wanted the beginning of the film to be in natural sound, and progressively for the sound to be more and more distorted (as my own hearing was in bondage). After about five minutes into the movie, the reverb kicks in and instead of a young woman moaning, you begin to hear the percussion of the sounds of traffic moving by outside the building. My moans become a sort of jungle beat. The sounds of reality melt into a nightmarish audio soup.

I suffer from nightmares to this day, but I don't know which are worse: the ones I have when I'm asleep or the ones I have when I am awake and trying to deal with this life. I know you know what I am talking about. If you want to see the movie, I think it's on the Internet somewhere. Otherwise, it's on BIKINI GIRL Volume 10, which was a video edition and is about two hours longs. I haven't screened this film many times for public audiences, but one time, there was a drunken dance party at Club 57 and I had the film run with a record playing on the stereo system — jungle sounds and drum rhythms. (My fancy soundtrack wasn't ready yet from the recording studio.)

Everyone had been socializing noisily before the film was playing. We couldn't get people to sit down to look at a movie, so we just ran it and projected it through the crowd. People came to attention quickly and took seats. After about six minutes of the movie you could have heard a pin drop save for the record being played. At the end of the ten minutes, the party broke up. The music and dancing never resumed. No one said anything to me, either. They were too stunned to congratulate me or say good-night. People just filed out. Party over! None of my friends from Club 57 ever said much to me about my "self-portrait in bondage." I think I really threw them all for a loop!

After this experience I realized film-making was out of my realm, technically. It's just too damned difficult! I've done some projects with a hand-held video camera since then, and that's a whole 'nother ball game. Video is direct and easy to get a grip on. Film is expensive, and the medium overall is elusive. Hard to get your muse to shine on film. Looking back on this project, of course I am glad I did it. The film was never accepted by the avant-guarde film crowd, and if I hadn't put it on my own video/magazine project and promoted it myself, no one would have seen it. Lack of recognition doesn't make a project less viable. I stand by what I did.

16. *House Submissive*

A lot of the fools (um, I mean, "clients") who'd telephone 23rd Street ("The Grand Central of Sleaze") would ask, "Do you have a house submissive?" And the phone girl would always answer, "Of course we have a house submissive! Her name is so-and-so." Detailed descriptions were seldom given out over the phone, as most of those who asked were "phone freaks" and would never keep the appointments they'd made. "I can't give out descriptions over the phone. Would you like to make an appointment?" the phone girl would always ask crisply. The client would give his first name (John was actually not too common — it was more often Joe) and select a time for his appointment. Three or four clients would be booked at the same time, since often, none of them showed up —phone girls played flimsy odds.

When the doorbell would finally, actually, really ring, we workers would snap sluggishly to attention, finish eating, apply fresh lipstick while chewing cheeks full of rice and beans, and tug up our sagging stockings. The client would wait in a small sitting area. When we, The Product, were ready, we'd be marched out into the hallway by the front door and made to stand at attention, whether we were dominants or submissives. The client would be fetched from the sitting area, and a hasty introduction would be made of each available female. The client would then be on the spot to make a selection. The brave ones who saw nothing to their liking said they'd "come back later" and wisely and hastily beat a retreat. The others, those cowards too cowed by the reality of the situation, were pressured into picking one of us luckless workers as their little playmates for the hour.

For a dominant session it was $60 for an hour. For submissive, it was $80 for 40 minutes, or $120 for an hour. No tipping took place unless the girl was a hustler. Hustlers were strongly discouraged, but a few, like Ania, were very good at it and made excellent money during each shift. I never forced anyone to tip; thus, I seldom received any gratuities. My "reward", if you could call it that, was a steady stream of repeat customers. I usually turned four tricks each four-hour shift. I figured a steady flow of tricks was worth more than a few twenties slipping my way. Management seemed to take my point of view, and I was kept on.

Not all of us workers were able to be "switchable", but I enjoyed the variety, so was glad to be either dominant or submissive. We didn't have anyone who was "strictly submissive" Even the most truly submissive among us, such as the purple-haired Szandora, enjoyed topping when she got the chance. It was a welcome relief to her from being spanked, ordered to suck, etc. We did have some women, like Morticia (she really called herself that!) who only did dominant scenes. Morticia had long, straight nearly-black hair, was thin and with a dancer's body, and seemed to be Hispanic, though she often dressed in Indian saris. Her voice was extremely masculine, and rumor had it she was a sex-change. I never found out the truth, but she did show me a picture of herself as a teenager, and in that picture, it did look like she had a moustache. She left us about eight months after I signed on and went to work for Belle de Jour, where sex wasn't included with the sessions. She claimed she was happier there.

Theoretically, we weren't supposed to have sex with our clients during dominant sessions. The most we could give them was "body worship", which made my flesh crawl. I hated to feel a strange man's tongue on my body. Nonetheless, I learned how to have a powerful clitoral orgasm by strapping a man down to the bed on his back, spread-eagle, putting a dog collar and leather hood on him, tying up his genitals, applying nipple clamps, then straddling his head from behind, smothering him and forcing him to poke his tongue out of the mouth-slit on that filthy leather hood, and stimulate my clit.

Sometimes I urinated a little, quite involuntarily, into his mouth, in my excitement. I would grasp his leather-clad head, grind my cunt into his face, and lightning would strike. No doubt, this was very unsafe sex, but I had a hard time resisting it. While atop his face, I could whip his erect, tied genitals with a riding crop, gently but with feeling. It wasn't until years later that I learned to reproduce these sexual thrills with a male partner in a "normal" way.

My feeling of isolation was great — that I could not achieve the height of pleasure without engaging in "sick" acts with strangers. I had no straight friends, and certainly no straight coworkers, I could really confide in. Every time I started a new series of talk therapy sessions, the shrink would come on to me and try to get me to have sex with him or her. I also knew a shrink who enjoyed telling me all the personal details of his clients' lives. He'd have me wait in his waiting room while his patients came and went, and then, while we were out in the evening having dinner (after a quick fuck on his fold-out foam mattress he kept in a closet), he'd tell me all about each one. "She's a top model, you know," he said about one rather ordinary-looking young lady who'd left his office in tears. "Earns great money. But she has a lot of problems. Her personal life is a mess." And then he'd go on to tell me why. I wasn't interested, and broke it off with him after a couple of months. Naturally, I wasn't pleased to be listening to this doctor chat with me about the problems of his clients, but most of the shrinks I've known like to tell all.

Another, a shrink I paid to see weekly while Henry was in the mental hospital and I was depressed, told me the sex games I played were a manifestation of my severe childhood arthritis, which had bound me to a wheelchair twice. "You arthritics need to make games out of pain and confinement," he once told me, then asked me if I was sexually attracted to him. I didn't answer. "Because if you are sexually turned on to me," he continued, "that would be perfectly normal." I told him, finally, that no, I wasn't attracted to him. I wrote him a check and walked out, never to return.

Being submissive to a stranger off the street is definitely scary, but you get used to it after while. I was dominant and had to be in charge all the time I was taking the Trick's money, giving it to the phone girl, noting the time my session began, and signing my initials to the sleazy guest register. Then, when I went back to the dusty cubicle, I knelt down and said, "Yes, Master?"

"Take off your clothes," they usually said. "Show me the `toys' you have for us to play with." These "masters" seldom brought any of their own equipment (I assume most were out on "shopping errands" or other legitimate business they'd explained away to their wives and partners), so they expected me to keep a supply of my own implements, for use upon myself.

Each female employee on 23rd Street, The Grand Central of Sleaze, had her own trunk, which was padlocked (but sometimes pilfered nonetheless, despite its being locked) in her absence. My own trunk was always a mess, and had a lot of rope, condoms, Tiger Balm, candles, leather cuffs and collars, whips, ball gags, hoods, stockings, rubber attire, and a few changes of costume in it, among other things. I'd go and fetch things from my trunk in the hallway. Often, I was naked. My sister co-workers didn't care, if they were on their way to the toilet or escorting a Trick to a cubicle, and spotted me nude, rummaging through my box of toys. I wasn't supposed to be seen by any other visiting clients in a nude state, but often, I was, and to a one, those Tricks who'd seen me prancing about in the buff would come back and pick me at some future date, to see what I was like. Just show a trick a naked whore, and chances are he'll be back later to get a little taste.

Most so-called "Masters" were rather confused by it all. They hadn't really thought things out in advance, so adopted "stern" attitudes, which were really laughable. It was hard to keep from smiling during these ridiculous "dominant" sessions. Of course, one had to appear dead serious, or there might be a whipping in the coming, more severe than was agreeable. I acted very calm (even when I was very afraid) and compliant, responding, "Yes, Master" to every order dished out. "What do you like, slave?" I was often asked. This was just what I wanted to hear, as I could then control and direct the session.

"I like to be spanked, Master," I'd reply, with seeming humbleness. "I need you to spank my naughty ass, gently, but repeatedly, until I am squirming from the pain." They usually took the cue, relieved that I was taking a part in managing the encounter.

"Okay, slave, on your stomach. Push that ass up into the air. Don't move!" they'd usually say. They'd usually fondle my posterior, brush their hands over my cunt, and touch and squeeze my small, dangling breasts.

Each time they'd strike me, whether I was ordered to do so or not, I'd reply, breathlessly, "One — thank you, Master. Two..." and so on. My gasps of pleasure weren't always faked. Those who had a gentle touch and who focused their flat-palmed blows on the very fleshy parts of my butt tended to actually arouse me. The first 30 or

40 spanks were pretty easy to take, but after that, I'd moan after each one. The more astute ones checked my pussy, which was usually getting wet by this point. I always placed a condom on the mattress in an obvious location. Once the client was aroused, I'd hear him rip open the condom, much to my relief, as I knew the session would soon be over. They seldom stuck around long after they'd come.

Penetration from behind, "doggie style", is difficult and one client later took advantage and raped me roughly and very quickly in this manner, damaging my female organs and putting me in a hospital for ten days after reconstructive surgery. It takes a lot of skill to allow a strange man, no matter how small he might be, to enter one from behind in this manner. The penetration tends to be very deep and painful. I knew a lot of women who worked at The Grand Central of Sleaze who just wouldn't do it doggie style — or who cried afterward.

After my ten days in the hospital, I was minus most of one ovary, and the other tattered ovary had been reconstructed. I stayed with my parents in Ohio for a week, and against doctor's orders, returned to New York. My mother had taken to getting drunk and accusing me of causing tension between herself and my father. Her voice would pitch low and she'd growl obscenities at me. When I got back to New York, I hoped my boyfriend (later to become my second husband) would move in and help take care of me during my convalescence, but he didn't. My straight job, at Harcourt Brace Jovanovich publishers, fired me. Apparently, my boss had walked out in a huff during my sick leave, and her bosses, in anger, had eliminated my job and hers altogether. The company was getting ready to relocate to Florida, and didn't offer to take me back and employ me after my month of sick leave. This wasn't the first time I was fired for being sick.

Back I went to 23rd Street, earlier than I should have done, but in desperate need of cash. My rent hadn't been paid. The surgeon sent me an enormous bill. Even though I should have been taking it easy, I was working nearly full-time on 23rd Street and doing sex during submissive sessions. I had a large scar on my abdomen that itched and was healing badly. It was the same cut as if I'd given birth Cesarian. I tried to cover it with panties, but the clients usually saw it. I don't know what they thought. They probably didn't think anything, as they proceeded to shove their penises up my cunt and into my mouth.

Out of the $80 for a 40 minute session, I got $40, but if I worked a half-shift I had to give $10 per evening to the "Hawkeye", and if I worked a full shift, or "double" as we called them, I owed $20 to the Hawkeye — but only if I turned at least one trick. The phone girl usually got 10 percent of the gross house take. Those phone girls worked from 10 or 11 in the morning until about 11 at night, and had to clean the place afterward. Very hard work for very little money. Of course, it was tax-free income. Some of the phone girls were on Welfare or had partners or spouses who worked straight jobs, so the cash they pulled in was just gravy. Like us girls "on the floor", many of the phone girls had substance abuse problems. They struggled to keep ahead of their habits and keep their rents paid.

Considering all the time and effort we, the staff, put into our sleazy labor, we earned very little. At least some money had to be spent on makeup, costumes, condoms, etc. If we broke a whip while beating a client, the client never reimbursed us so we could buy a new one. All of our equipment purchases came out of our individual wallets. I couldn't see much difference between my straight jobs and my kinky work. Either way, the money seemed to boil down to minimum wage. The only difference at my secretarial jobs during the day was that I was wearing clothes while men (my bosses) humiliated me. It was a rare pleasure when I saw a client who wanted a "switchable" session. I always proposed that he'd dominate me first for 20 minutes, then I'd dominate him for 20 minutes. My pleasure was often genuine when I'd be allowed to turn the tables and administer a riding crop to the butt of the guy who had just been slapping me around and pinching me.

Szandora (I knew her real first and last name, but won't repeat it here) was one of the few workers at The Grand Central of Sleaze who truly enjoyed being submissive. It was in her blood. So were a few other things. She liked to receive champagne enemas, and in general, to be penetrated anally (something I've never been able to tolerate, myself). She drank quite a bit. Her trick was to mix some cheap whiskey in with Coke in a big plastic liter bottle, and drink that all day. Her eyes were often very red. She'd do almost any drug she could get her hands on, but seemed to enjoy injecting cocaine the most of any high. Before long, her veins collapsed. She couldn't get a fix and would cry in frustration, blood dripping all over her bathroom. (She lived in the neighborhood, and I visited her at home a few times.)

Despite her problems, Szandora was a very sweet person, and absolutely reliable to lend money to. She constantly hit you up for very small loans, such as $2. Her credit and reputation were so good with drug dealers downtown, she could actually buy such small amounts of drugs as two dollars a buy, as she was a daily client. She was absolutely scrupulous about returning the $2 you'd lent her, and just as soon as possible, because she needed to be able to ask you a few days later for another loan. She kept a very clean credit rating. She had to. She began to plot to get out of New York, but it was too late. She was hospitalized for about 60 days with inflammation of the heart, something that often strikes people who shoot coke. In her case, however, her recovery was insignificant. It soon became evident she was HIV positive. I heard she moved to Arizona and took a live-in childcare position with a family, but that in the absence of drugs, she'd taken to drinking to excess. Then, I didn't hear anything about her for a long time, since I'd retired from The Life in January 1984, and my contacts were few and far between with my former co-workers. In 1993, I finally found out Szandora had died of AIDS. I don't know when or where, exactly. I don't know where any of my former co-workers are. I miss some of them a lot, and wish we could have stayed in touch, but things just don't go like that in The Life.

17. *Turning Tricks At Home*

Engaging in flat-out, pay-by-the-hour prostitution is never something I've ever recommended to anyone, friend or foe. You'll quickly come to the attention of the police, or worse. Your neighbors will harass you, you'll be evicted, the list of headaches is endless. Where I live now in Europe, prostitution itself isn't illegal, but back in New York, where I lived for about 17 years, it was and still is darned illegal. I didn't let anyone into my apartment unless I'd checked them out carefully. Then, I'd seldom charge an hourly fee for the encounter. Since I'm into kinky stuff for fun, I'd try to make it a "barter" arrangement, hoping to steer free of legal hassles. (I always have.) Two adults can meet in New York and pretty much do as they please if the only things involved are "gifts", such as dinner, drinks, and trinkets. This is more widely known as "dating." If sex occurs by mutual consent, and it's done behind closed doors, that's the business of the two adults. One hopes.

I was always very nervous, letting people know where I lived and letting them into my place. For many years I was married or had a live-in partner, and home encounters weren't available, but when I was single in New York, such as in 1994, I had Don visit a

lot. Don is approaching middle age, has worked for the government, has a law degree, and though he usually has a straight girlfriend or two or three, he is so seriously kinky he won't marry until
he finds the Woman of his Wet Dreams. I applaud him. I've rushed
into marriage three times, and the first two were terrible mistakes.
If you're out there and still single and want to couple up, please
don't hurry. Especially if you're kinky. My first husband was way
too kinky and wild for me. My second wasn't kinky enough. The
third — everything is going well so far, our fourth year together.
He cross-dresses and isn't afraid to pierce himself. My kinda guy.

Don orders slutty outfits from Frederick's of Hollywood for
himself to wear, and gets his shoes from Lee's Mardi Gras in New
York. He's not a transvestite per se: he cross-dresses to emphasize
his submissiveness, he says. To make himself feel more humble and
silly. I enjoy his frilly costumes, his dressing up. He keeps a bachelor apartment in New York, with all his S/M equipment carefully
packed into a trunk he stashes under his bed. He keeps a collection
of cowboy hats, which hangs from racks on the wall. When I go to
visit him, he takes down the hat collection and replaces it with
whips, paddles, cuffs, hoods, costumes, etc. The music is turned
up a little so the neighbors can't hear as well, and the games begin.
He bought me a cute leather cocktail dress. He has other things for
me to wear, if I want a change of costume. I could keep any of
these costumes — they are mine for the asking. He is very generous. Last year, he sent me some cash toward buying a washing
machine, although he lives in the United States and I live in

Europe, and we see each other very seldom these days. Often, I'd show up at Don's apartment and we'd do a session together.

When his ass was nice and sore from my prolonged spankings and whippings and his dick had been whipped almost to the bleeding point (but not quite), we'd go to Minetta's Tavern in the Village and chow down. He loves food and drink and money is no object. Don liked my current husband immediately, and vice versa. They are both happy to remain in their own realms and relate to me on an individual basis. Very fair. I remember one evening Don came over to my place in Brooklyn, while my husband was there. Don showed up around 8:00 p.m. with wine and Ricard for us to drink. I smoked a joint or two. My husband mostly stayed in the other room, but came out from time to time to snap a picture of my scene with Don. As long as Don gets a print of the photo, and his face isn't showing, he doesn't mind being photographed at all.

I began the session in my usual way: I make the slave wear a collar and leash, and if possible, a hood. I restrain his hands (in this case, they were cuffed behind his back) and kneel before me, and lick my shoes, all over, including the soles of course, until they are very wet. A ball gag may then be stuffed into his mouth and securely affixed. I next have the slave kneel before me, while I hold the leash and a riding crop, and I gently press my high-heeled fetish heels into his growing hard-on. I may then quietly order the slave to perform a number of pleasurable and humiliating acts for me.

"You're going to do everything I say, right, slave?"

"Yes, Mistress." The slave is permitted to look at my legs,

body and face before being transferred to his next position (usually to receive a spanking); after that, it is likely he will be blindfolded, to increase his feelings of helplessness. I light candles to create atmosphere, burn incense, and play whatever music pleases me that particular evening. As a slave's cock gets hard, I carefully tie it with a very long leather thong, putting the slave penis into intricate bondage, very careful not to tear the delicate genital skin. The pain intensifies due to the increasing stiffness of the slave cock against the unyielding cord. Nipple clamps are usually applied, though if a slave is new at the game, I merely squeeze and stimulate the slave's nipples with my leather gloves on. I often put the kid gloves under the slave's nose, for him to sniff. Most slaves are intoxicated by the smell of leather. The nipple torture helps to establish trust. I take slaves as far as they can go without making them cry, without breaking the skin. When their precious little cocks are not torn by my ministrations, this ensures further respect and tremendous gratitude on their parts. My spankings always begin gently, and I allow a slave to grind his genitals into my leather-clad lap or across my bare thighs. Often, the penis will begin to lubricate. "Naughty slave," I whisper, not at all angry at the signs of their arousal.

(I usually ask the slave to crawl away and fetch a towel for my lap to absorb any penis lube, before the spanking continues. As much as there is the pleasing prospect of dinner, drinks and gifts, there is the exciting aspect of doing something so naughty in my home, with a relative stranger. Again I stress, I usually check out people very carefully before I let them visit where I live or go to see them. We correspond a long time, talk on the phone, and often go on a "normal" drinks date before a relationship is allowed to develop. Except to experiment, I've never done hard drugs, and don't welcome slaves who did. Don wouldn't even smoke a joint with me. He is only into kinky sex and fine wines.)

During the first couple of years I knew him, I only made Don come (ejaculate) one time. He was very excited — I'd worked him all over, including anally — and I gave him a sort of hand job with a big metal vibrator, until he squirted all over his own belly. His orgasms are not very important to me, but I do like seeing a slave penis squirt. It's not up to me to make slaves have orgasms, just to try to provide the setting for acting out their fantasies — and mine. Of course, I hope they ejaculate, but that is incidental.

As for myself, the pleasures are more subtle. Dinner, drink, smoke, and useful, practical gifts are appealing to me. The power I have over slaves, both males and female (I have slaves of both sexes, and also gender-blurred slaves), the power to charm and entice them — that gives me a good feeling. If you say I am crazy because I do not charge Don thousands of dollars to visit him or let him visit me at my place, I say to hell with you. What Don has given me is worth a lot of money. In fact, without even being asked to, he has given me hundreds of dollars in cash.

In late 1993, after I left my second husband, I was homeless while I waited six weeks for an apartment I'd sublet to become available. I often bathed and slept at Don's house. He brought me the dinners I asked for — usually a selection from the local salad bar — and we'd talk and look at videos until I fell asleep. I cleaned myself again in the morning and left feeling fresh — and safe. When I got pregnant and had a near miscarriage and abortion to clear it up, I got fired from my New York Wall Street job. Don came to the rescue to cheer me up with Chinese takeout food (my favorite!) and cash. I felt better. We've declared ourselves "friends for life" We both like fishing and always wanted to take a fishing trip together, but never did.

I met Don through a personals ad. Carter Stevens had an S/M contact magazine going, and I submitted a personals ad to him, which he ran for free as both a courtesy to me and for the handling fees he'd collect from all interested slaves who responded to my ad. I got about 200 letters from that ad — I answered them all, too. (It was a lot of work!) But the first letter, the very first one I opened and answered, was from Don. Fate! We met for drinks at Fanelli's bar in SoHo. Although I was sick with the flu, we leaned on the bar, had whiskies, and chatted as loud as we pleased about all the fun we'd had in the S/M scene. Quite a few patrons around us were openly eavesdropping on our conversation. Don said the jealousy on some of their faces was obvious.

"I like you. I pick you. I'm gonna quit while I'm ahead," I said, toasting him.

"I'm so happy I answered that ad right away," he smiled. "I never thought I had a chance to meet you!" That was the beginning of a beautiful friendship. Don has tried to get me to interest some of my straight girlfriends into our kinky relationship — to make it a threesome. I have tried, but I have always failed. The ladies I selected to join in on our little scene have always shied away. I got the farthest with Rowan, who went out with us for dinner at Minetta's Tavern one night, and declared, "Lisa, you should fall in love with this guy. You two are perfect together!" A few years later she even accompanied us to an S/M-theme restaurant in Manhattan, and then to an S/M private club. She had a good time, and we enjoyed her company, but clearly, she is not into the scene as we are.

I stay in touch with Don, and he has a standing invitation to come visit me in Europe — even to bring his fishing poles! I never know when we'll ever see one another. I'm glad I took the chance and let him get to know me personally, on a semi-professional basis. To be my friend, and my slave.

I am certainly not sure I could recommend this type of relationship to most people. It wouldn't work for many. A lot of kinky hookers would need and want to be paid their hourly fee and wouldn't like the casual way I deal with slaves (sometimes they give me cash, sometimes they do not). A lot of slaves would need to pay me cash, in order to keep that needed distance, to keep things formal and strictly money-based. Once things get informal and friendship sets in, a lot can go wrong.

18. *Pen Pals and Other Friends Via Mail*

Debbie D is a model, singer and actress who works in the Philadelphia area. She does a lot of specialty posing for individual clients, via the mail. I don't custom-model by mail or in person as much as I used to, so I have referred some of my former clients to Debbie. I enjoy keeping in touch with her by mail. She's the new generation of custom model. Nice to know what the kids are up to these days.

She's a "scream queen" — she appears in lots of low-budget, shot-on-video horror and action movies. She's not the greatest actress, that's for sure, but she's got a body that won't quit. She usually wins awards at the Mermaid Parade at Coney Island every year, and has a variety of mermaid, vampire, and even vampire/mermaid costumes and French maid/vampire get-ups, all custom-made of course, sequined, and very fancy. I can't really figure out why anyone would want to pretend they are both a mermaid and a vampire, but it all seems logical to Debbie, who sometimes speaks of her dedication to "the blue rose" I don't get it at ALL when she starts talking about that "blue rose", but getting it doesn't seem very important, somehow.

I started having pen pals at a tender age. One of the nerdi-est and most annoying of hobbies, to be sure. I've had one pen pal since I was about 15! I've even met him once. He lives in Virginia and is a really nice guy. We swap music tapes and gossip. It does-n't seem so stupid if you're lonely and you establish true friendships by mail. Maybe it's a little bit sad, but I don't think there's any-thing intrinsically wrong with it. My favorite pen pals are the ones who'll swap naughty snapshots with me. Herein lies the gray area — it's no longer "innocent" correspondence. I realize that swap-ping dirty photos by mail is very childish, but I just love sending nude photos of myself to people in, say, Slovakia, and getting back photos of them playing with their genitals! Sue me!

I have one pen pal in Scandinavia whose rubber-clad hus-band plays the slave, and she plays the raincoat-clad mistress. She has several thousand raincoats in a special room they built in the attic of their house. Rubber, plastic, vinyl — any raincoat will do. She puts one on, ties her husband under a special toilet made of plexiglass, and pisses on him while he jerks off. You can't make this stuff up! Most of my pen pals have standing invitations to visit me, but the visits seldom happen. A few of my best pen pals are incar-cerated, too, making visits impossible. I went to meet a penpal in England twice. I'd met him once before, when he was visiting New York. He'd been the boyfriend of a girlfriend of mine, and I liked him, so stayed in touch with him after they broke up. Not long after I visited him the first time, he stripped nude and commandeered a double-decker bus. He was locked up for quite awhile after that episode — a combination prison/mental hospital. Last time I saw him, six years later, he seemed much better, but about a year after that, I got an angry letter from him about God and the Devil, and he threatened to sue me for slander, of all things. For what, I never figured out. Most pen pals fall by the wayside sooner or later...

I found all three of my husbands through the mail. I do mail-art and publish a 'zine (BIKINI GIRL) sporadically. The first husband, I actually met in an S/M club, but it was my magazine and mail-art activities that made him propose to me seven days after our meeting. Talk about a whirlwind romance! My second husband submitted some writing to my 'zine. Despite the fact that I suspected he was mentally ill, we married a few years later, and stayed together a total of 11 years. My current husband sent me amazing fan letters from Europe and American cash to subscribe to BIKINI GIRL. He took one look at the 'zine and decided I was going to be his wife — even though I was already married, and was having an affair. He wrote to me and asked me to marry him. I dashed off a note saying I would, then promptly forgot about it. (He showed me the letter later, to remind me. Sure enough, I'd done it! But it's Zsa Zsa Gabor's fault! She advises to always say yes to marriage, even if you're already married! I blame it on Zsa Zsa!)

Husband Three then began to chant homemade magickal spells, remaining confident I would leave everything behind and run to Europe to be with him. I guess his magick spells were effective! Or maybe it was those amazing fan letters he sent me about my 'zine. He is ten years my junior, and a cross-dresser. Whether

or not I've made the right choice by marrying Husband Three, I
can surely swear, it's never a dull moment.

Correspondence is the medium of the truly lonely. I can
write page after page and assemble packages of photos and clippings for my favorite pen pals, but don't have to actually go outside and meet anyone face to face (except to stand in line at the
Post Office). I have a few penpals I know so little about, I don't
even know their real names or addresses. I am so shy, I don't usually press them for facts about themselves. If they don't want to tell
me more about themselves, send me a snapshot of themselves,
whatever, I guess that's okay with me. It's almost more fun to imagine what they look like.

The entire realm of bizarre correspondence fascinates me. I
have a compilation of BIZARRE magazine by John Willie, and
love reading the bizarre letters section! Of course, some seem to
have been obviously written and answered by Mr. Willie himself.
He was quite a strange guy. I wonder who will write his biography?
I'd love to read it. It could be made into a movie, starring Johnny
Depp! I once saw an original print (very rare) of a photo he himself had taken of his wife, Holly. If I get the story straight, they
lived in Australia together, and she was the model for Sweet
Gwendoline, only brunette in real life. In the photo I saw of her,
she was completely nude (except for, I think, black kid gloves up
to the elbows, but perhaps my memory fails me on this point), and
she was cuffed by the wrists and the ankles, and there was a chain
between the two points. She was wearing extremely high fetish

heels. Further, the gossip I heard was that she was the kinkier of the two in the couple, and got John into experimenting. She was, by all accounts, a "true submissive", and couldn't get enough of being tied up or posing for her husband. She interests me. I wonder when she died? And where? Does anyone know? I think John committed suicide. The part of their personal story that interests me the most is that, apparently, she was so very submissive, it freaked him out and he ran. Do you think this is plausible? I do. If anyone knows the truth, please contact me via the publisher.

I have a large collection of snapshots I've received through the mail over the years. Almost to a one, they are "softcore" — no penetration goes on. But they are definitely "dirty."

I continue to have pen pals and to exchange photos with people by the mail. I can certainly recommend Debbie D as a source of photos — she has sent me dozens of them these past few years. I only subscribed to her fan club once, that I can recall, but she keeps on mailing me stuff. I have pictures of her smiling, laughing and in motion, holding her waistlength hair out of the way to better show off her lovely back and buttocks, and I remember a hundred private photo sessions I did myself for amateur photogs. As I look back on it all, I know it was immoral, but I needed the extra money to take care of myself. What do you think I should have done? Gone back to my parents and demand they care for me? Maybe I should have. I wish they had been more helpful with my undergraduate studies, but in my heart of hearts, I do not think parents have much obligation to their children financially past the age of 18. In Europe, where I live now, children often live at home until they marry, but this isn't done anymore much in the U.S. I've never had children of my own, so can't point any fingers or pontificate. At the same time that I am proud that I left home at 18 and fended for myself, I feel shame that I fell into prostitution to fund my college studies. If I have any money to leave when I am dead, I will do my level best to donate it to one scholarship fund or another. I would like to get rich and establish a fund specifically for kids who have wandered into The Life to pay for university studies (to help keep them out of The Life). I have no one but some distant relatives and in-laws to leave anything to. It would do my soul good, I think, to know I might keep just one young person out of prostitution and further their education. What do you think? Am I foolish to think that by saving just one, it will make a difference?

In no way do I want to encourage young people to engage in prostitution or bondage modeling, as I have done. I put myself at tremendous risk, and obviously, my family must feel shame at my actions. I am not close to my blood relatives, but I wouldn't want to hurt their feelings. I hope anyone who has ever known me can forgive my transgressions and understand why I am writing this book.

I take another look at Debbie D. Look at that butt! Does she have a figure or what? Should she hide that, or should she expose herself? She never does hardcore. She teases. I like it. I find it aesthetically pleasing. I never get tired of looking at Debbie, and I remember posing for myself, vainly, in front of a mirror when I was young. Is vanity wrong? Yes and no. Selfish vanity is wrong, but appreciation for oneself is not. If you know you are good-looking, and you like having your picture taken, why shouldn't you have your picture taken? One of Jeffrey Dahmer's victims was, as his relatives termed it, "a photo fanatic", and would pose for anyone interested. And that "photo fanatic" met a horrible fate. I try to contemplate the horror of Jeffrey Dahmer's murderous acts, and all I can think of is, "He came from Northeastern Ohio, same as I did. He looks like some of my cousins" Somehow, I can understand his frustration and murderous impulses, but it is impossible to elaborate upon this. Perhaps I am sick, as he was. If you are very straight, you are probably thinking, "Of course, you are very sick, Lisa." And I would understand your attitude if I met you. But I cannot seem to place myself either in the role of victim or aggressor. My past, my very life, seems to lie firmly in gray areas.

What would you do if you had a daughter like me?

I wish I could sit with my own parents and brother and talk for hours and hours about all that water under the bridge. But my parents are elderly now and are in poor health, and my brother is far off and has problems of his own. It's too late for me to heal my family. In fact, why should I see myself as the healer? In my own family, am I the one best equipped to take charge and do the healing?

19. *Homeless*

For the last six weeks of 1993, I was homeless. I had often heard the term "homeless" and felt pity for those unfortunates who had ended up in that condition, but couldn't bring myself to understand the concept of homelessness very much. I mean, how does one end up losing one's home? I just didn't get it. Had those homeless people foolishly gotten themselves dwellings they couldn't afford? Had they been stupid enough not to save six month's worth of living expenses put aside for a rainy day? I struggled to comprehend and have compassion for their plights. I have heard it said that most Americans are only two paychecks away from homelessness. That wasn't the case with me. One of my first projects in New York was to save $1,000, and I kept building on that savings account until, along with my second husband, we had about $90,000 put away. They say you should always have six month's worth of living expenses put aside. I was so paranoid, I took it to the max! Even with my relatively high-priced New York City lifestyle, ninety grand could have sustained me for several years if I'd played it cool. Ninety grand! (Wish I had it now!)

I usually worked straight jobs, and although some of my checks bounced over the years, that was just due to bad math, not malicious intent. I never had an apartment worth more than about 25 per cent of my monthly income. When I married a second time and my then-husband began selling pulp fiction, we got a second apartment in the same neighborhood in Brooklyn, so he could "have his own space." This inspired an incredible amount of jealousy among my so-called "friends" We had two of everything: two kitchens, two bathrooms, two living rooms, two home offices, two telephone numbers. And both places were so reasonably priced, I was able to pay the bills on time each month. I had plenty of personal space and so did my second husband, and we acquired possessions at a fast pace. (Why is it that we rushed to fill up the space? Why do people do that????) Childless, we not only had our own apartments and separate incomes, we were able to spend so much time apart from one another, I began to lead a double life! I took another "husband" in Manhattan, who only knew one of my addresses and one of my telephone numbers. When I told him I was separated from my second husband, he believed me; after all, when he visited once for a weekend, he saw only some of my husband's clothes — no evidence of the husband himself. (Because my second husband was spending the weekend in "his" apartment, just a few blocks away.)

This double life went on for several years. As far as I know, the two men will only know of one another through publication of this book. But maybe they both knew all along. I had two "husbands" — one I was legally married to, the other was a lover — at the same time. I met my "legal" second husband in 1980, began dating him in 1982, and promptly fell hopelessly in love. We married in 1985. Almost immediately, he stopped fucking me. Upon marriage, he no longer felt the urge for the pursuit, for the raw excitement of animalistic sex, which we'd had plenty of before we got married. When I complained, he told me there were more important things in life than sex. "Yeah, like what?" I asked. He had no answer. I mean, isn't sex supposed to be one of those cool benefits of marriage? Hey — you are legally entitled to fuck each other's brains out! It's cool! It's fun! You only have to stop to get up and pee and shop for food and eat and go to work sometimes, right? Why should sex have to stop after marriage? Shouldn't there be a passionate free-for-all for at least a few years, until things simmer down? And even then, shouldn't there be an occasional wonderful quickie on the kitchen floor?????

I was faithful for six years before I took the second "husband." What a joy it was to finally have orgasms again! I lost weight, got my hair done, and wore makeup and perfume every day. I felt pretty. I felt wanted. I felt sexy again. In 1993, the lover asked me to marry him. What a dilemma! I already was married! I gave him a definite "maybe", then did my own divorce, paying a local attorney about four hundred dollars to make sure I filled out the forms correctly and filed them in the right order. In the Fall of 1993, I took a trip to Paris (I'd always wanted to go there) with my "legal" second husband, who had no idea how close I was to walking out on him once and for all. On this trip to Paris, I met the young man who was to become my third husband. Smitten, I returned to New York, broke up with the lover, and told the second husband I was divorcing him. Shocked, he signed the papers. Mute.

The year before, when my insurance business had failed and money got really tight, I had frugally given up "my" apartment, a rent-stabilized one-bedroom on Prospect Park Southwest, threw out the "second of everything" (or had given it to charity), and moved in with my second husband. The lover and I had temporarily broken up, anyway. I quit drinking and sank into deep depression. No sex + no alcohol = sad Lisa. I tried to coexist with my second husband until my divorce was final and until my rent-stabilized apartment, which I'd wisely sublet, was free again, but couldn't stomach sleeping in the same bed with Husband Two anymore.

On November 11, 1993, 13 years to the day (completely by chance, I swear) after I walked out on my first husband, I said goodbye to Husband Two and headed for Manhattan — a place I've always felt at home in. Then, I spent the next six weeks homeless. I pulled out my address books and called everyone I knew, asking to sleep only one night on their couches and to be able to take a shower before I left in the morning. The only thing holding my life together was my job as an account executive at a financial public relations firm. When the work day would end, since I had nowhere to go, I'd call the deli from my desk and order up my usual dinner: a quart of beer, a container of cottage cheese, and a buttered roll. I'd work on my accounts until 8 or 9 p.m. My boss was bewildered, but the clients were happy with my work and one even wrote me an unsolicited letter of commendation. I got a raise. I'd make phone calls from the office all day, arranging a place to crash for the night.

Around 9:30 p.m. I'd head to a friend's apartment, lie down on their couch and sleep, usually in my clothes. In the morning, I'd shower and wash my hair, change underwear, have a cup of coffee, and be back off to Midtown and the public relations firm. I had a Post Office box and checked it daily, looking for love letters from Paris from the young French guy with whom I was smitten. When I'd find a letter from him, I'd dash into a Blarney Stone-type bar near Grand Central, sit and have a bladder cocktail (vodka and cranberry juice), and smoke a hand-rolled cigarette of Amsterdamer pipe tobacco. On my breaks, I'd drench myself in Fahrenheit for Men by Dior, trying hard to imagine I was back in Paris with my adored 26year old anorexic chain-smoking cheese-eater, who still lived with his parents and worked selling screws. The hand-rolled cigarettes were his brand. The perfume, although for men, reminded me of his scent. I WAS HEAD OVER HEELS IN LOVE AND DIDN'T KNOW WHAT THE FUCK I WAS DOING.

For the first full two weeks of homelessness, it was fun and I actually had a good time with it all. It was like two weeks of camping out, or two weeks of pyjama parties (without the pyjamas). I still had the keys to my second husband's apartment, and visited once or twice a week to change clothes, do my laundry,

cook us both a hot meal, and make sure he was shopping for groceries for himself, feeding our cat, and keeping his bills paid.

As Thanksgiving approached, I got an invitation to join an
unmarried couple I knew for the big feast. "No thanks," I said. I
went to visit my second husband and arrived with a cartload of
groceries and proceeded to stuff and roast a turkey, get drunk,
watch the parade on TV, and serve a meal for eight for only two
people — all the trimmings. It was, despite the circumstances of
the impending divorce, a pleasant day. I even slept there that night.
"Stay on your own side of the bed," I warned him.

During my six weeks of homelessness, my employer knew
my marriage was breaking up and that I was waiting for my sublet
apartment to become available again so I could move back in. My
boss called me a whore and when he'd pat my shoulders, his hands
would linger. He'd stand very close to me and ask a lot of questions
about the phantom "husband" I had abandoned, and if the guy in
Paris was a good lover or not. "I don't know," I replied. "I haven't
tried him yet." I couldn't think of a snappier retort, like "Fuck
you." I needed the job and let the boss bully and harass me.

I'd always felt the East Village was my living room, so I
moved easily in that neighborhood while homeless. I knew all the
nicest restaurants where they had superclean spacious toilets,
working payphones, and you could get a big bowl of homemade
soup for a couple of bucks. I got extra bread on the side when I
frankly told them about my situation. I ate sitting at bars, and
treated myself to individual glasses of champagne. Just because I

was homeless didn't mean I had to drink water!

After two weeks, the novelty of my self-imposed homelessness had vanished. I was plain ol' dog tired. I was hyper-vigilant — every step of my day had to be planned in advance. How many days would it be before I could get fresh changes of clothes? Where had I left my dry cleaning to have done? Had I lost the ticket? The weather had turned very cold. I had to keep covered up and be sure to eat, to keep up my flagging strength. I thought I had a hundred or so reliable friends. Suddenly, they were all out of town or simply refused, point blank, a night's hospitality. Many of these were people who still owed me money! I got a nasty taste of reality soup during this period of time. People I'd actually sheltered, people whose clothes I'd washed, people whom I'd fed chicken dinners, were suddenly on their way overseas and couldn't even lend me their spaces to crash in for a single night. On the other hand, some people I barely knew rallied and invited me over for repeat visits. It was shocking to find out who my true friends were.

One friend, a woman, had always encouraged me to leave Husband Two, and had a standing offer of a free place to stay for two weeks if I ever did. When I left him, she sounded shocked, avoided me for a few weeks, then finally let me sleep over one night. She gave me a suit of clothes to wear that no longer fit her, a new toothbrush, a bagel and coffee in the morning, and I was shown the door, not to see her again for years. Our friendship of more than a decade suddenly seemed not to count at all. I went to church chapels and lit candles and prayed a lot, putting coins in the charity boxes. I gave quarters to beggars in the subway. Anything to turn my karma around! By week three I was bone-tired, and made up my mind that people who chose to live as hoboes were out of their damned minds. Life is nothing but pain when you don't have a hot bath every day, a complete change of clean clothes, a safe place to leave your possessions, and a soft, decent bed to sleep in, even if it's just a mattress on the floor. (I still sleep on a mattress on the floor at this writing. Hard on the back, but I can snuggle under the blankets and press myself up against Husband Three if I get cold at night.)

The last day of December, the woman I'd sublet my apartment to moved out, having found another apartment in the same building. New Year's Day, 1994, I hired some friends and a van to help me move my things out of my second husband's place. The van broke down and needed about $600 worth of work. By late that day, I was in the new space, too tired to find the sheets to put on my just-delivered Dial-A-Mattress. The former subtenant had left me a TV set to borrow for a few days, with cable hookup. I ordered a pizza and soda and, shocked,sat on the floor in my old bedroom and watched "Married With Children" I called my second husband, to let him know I'd safely arrived. I immediately started crying. "Forgive me!" I moaned, then hung up.

For the next couple of weeks, I was too unraveled to unpack the boxes. Angelo, my slave, came over and got me away from the vodka bottle long enough to pick out some old artwork to have freshly framed and hung, and he painstakingly unpacked my things and arranged them in the apartment, which suddenly seemed very big.

When the homelessness first began, the first place I called was The Grand Central of Sleaze, which by this time had moved to 28th Street (just down the block from the place owned by my first husband — another S/M brothel). I asked for my old job back, and was given it immediately. I worked two weeknights each week, plus all day and night Sunday. It was such a cold winter, much of the city shut down, and in five months I earned next to nothing. In fact, the cold knocked out our phones on many nights, and often I had to borrow $20 from management to get to a latenight deli, buy some canned spaghetti and beer, and ride the train all the way out to Brooklyn at one in the morning — not even having enough money for a safer, faster cab ride. A few nights, I had absolutely no place to go. I could have used a credit card for a cheap hotel room, but a cheap hotel room in New York is an ugly place, indeed. Anyway, I was nearly twenty thousand dollars in debt on my various credit cards. I wanted to cash in on all the debts I imagined my so many "friends" owed me. What a rude shock — I discovered I had very few friends indeed, and as I've already said, most seemed to be packing up to move to Mongolia for a few years and couldn't entertain to save their lives. It felt strange and sad, to say the least, to be back in The Life after a full nine years of absence. What was scarier was that a few of my former co-workers were still in the biz, but worse, I saw tricks I hadn't seen in nearly a decade. There they were, still buying whores in New York City!

I don't have a "standard session" I offer, but if a slave isn't sure what he wants, I do have a certain repertoire I rely upon to use up the sixty minute session. After they are "completely comfort-able" (nude) I return, ask what they have in mind, agree on a price, collect the money, and turn it in to the phone girl. I then have my last chance to pee or finish eating my dinner. Then, when I enter the session room, the meter is running. I like to make a slave kneel on my chain belt (intensely painful — have you tried it?) and count to 100 slowly, aloud, while I arrange the room and get ready. Then, I ask him to pick up the belt with his teeth and bring it to me, on his knees, hands behind his back (not tied). The belt weighs about seven pounds — it's not easy to transport in the teeth. I then take the belt, fasten it around my waist, and put a dog collar and leash on the slave. A big, black, thick slave collar with spikes on it. I take the leash in my hand, and give the slave a reas-suring smile, or at the very least, a calm face, to let them know I am not on drugs and am in control of things.

"You will address me as Mistress," I say to the slave.

"Yes, Mistress," is the required response. While they kneel at attention, with hands behind the back, I prod their growing hard-ons with my shiny red patent leather six-inch heels. I enjoy press-ing the spike heels gently so as not to cause damage into the tender flesh of slave-testicle. It is only the menace I seek. Pain is not need-ed at this moment. I wear elbowlength black kid gloves, and tweak and arouse the slave's nipples. I gently stroke and touch the geni-tals, making it clear I am a gentle Mistress but that the slave's body is mine for a full hour. There is no crevasse or cranny that is private to the slave during the session. I may wish to examine between their toes! The slave has to let me peek or prod where I please.

It is very difficult, as you can imagine, to take men off the street and create a sixty minute session for cut-rate prices with no tipping, involving sadism. My approach is to remain calm and not to put on a falsely stern face. I smile easily and chat and laugh freely with the clients. "What's a nice Jewish boy like you doing in a place like this?" I asked a lot of yarmulke-wearing customers. It certainly breaks the ice. Usually, these people have partners or wives. I meet very few who are completely alone — or so they tell me (tricks love to lie to whores). They always seem to have "a wife who doesn't care", but my suspicion is that they just haven't properly broached the subject with their partner. I mean, if you have a loving partner and you have a fantasy, couldn't you delicately approach the subject and try to inspire a fantasy in the head of your loved one? Something the two of you could share?

I want to digress for a minute and tell you what a lover did to me which made me feel worse than any chippie. Like many men, he had a desire to be penetrated anally. Okay, no big deal. A lot of males, even if they don't want downright penetration, do want their tushies touched and cooed over, and their testicles stroked, and the outer region of the asshole touched or possibly tongued. My lover had such a fantasy, and one night, he mutely turned his back to me, bent over, and insisted I penetrate his asshole with my fingers while masturbating him with my free hand.

Frankly, he looked ridiculous bent over like that, and this bad experience, which I blame on him, basically killed my feelings for him. I mean, why couldn't he have built me up to this over dinner or a cocktail? And if he wanted to use me as a chippie, why couldn't he call me "Mistress" and offer me a hundred dollar bill? This would have made a tolerable masquerade of the whole encounter. But, no — I was his lover, and so he expected me to service him gratis as he desired, even though he knew, for example, I like to have my pussy licked, and he only did it once or twice to me in all the time I knew him. (And yes, I do keep very clean, thank you.) In other words, he was never willing to give tit for tat. By treating me as he did, he turned me off. Remember this if you want to encourage your partner in fun and games! Try to stimulate some fantasy in them you both can share in, albeit from different perspectives. Your wife or girlfriend might enjoy being your "Venus in Furs" with real or fun furs, diamonds or lavishly tacky rhinestones, or at the very least, slavish personal pampering. (Yeah!)

My current husband asks to brush my waistlength hair almost every weekend. What a pleasure, to feel the brush stimulating my scalp! And he loves to see the dark blonde hair falling neatly as he unknots it. It seems to "do something" for him. Find out what your honey likes, and if you have a fantasy, try to build on it — gently.

Getting back to my slave session, I usually make the slave tongue-clean my shoes, tops and bottoms. Since the shoes are never worn in the street, few men object to this indignation. I carefully tie up their penises with a long leather thong, taking time so as not to tear the skin but sure to cause great pain as their hard-ons burgeon. Usually, clothespins clamp their nipples, and I take them over my knees, giving a very prolonged and gentle spanking. It's not hitting hard that counts — it's the repeat blows. If they squirm a little and get hard, I say nothing, unless their genitals are lubricating heavily. If that's the case, I scold them and make them go fetch a towel. I then often tie them face-up spread-eagle on the bed, and pretend to smother them under my fat butt, while caressing their cocks with a riding crop. I untie them, tie them face down spread-eagle, and give a light whipping to their buttocks. After indulging various of their fantasies, if they've specified them, I make them kneel before me and jerk off onto a paper towel on the floor, then help me tidy up the room. Are you shocked? Or did you just enjoy reading about what I do to naughty slaves like you? Confess!

This chapter has taken me through various memories, very scattershot. I'm not sure I've achieved the objective the chapter title indicates and talked much about homelessness. Surely, I haven't suffered all that much, only being without a home for six weeks a few years ago. It could have been worse. But it was a terrible experience, nonetheless, which took place during a domestic crisis (divorce), and I hope my telling of my homelessness gives you some insight and empathy toward homeless people in general. I hope you will give to charities, but more than that, I hope we all will work to reach out to our friends and neighbors when they have turmoil in their lives. If someone has a substance abuse problem, get them into a program — or something! There comes a time when we all have to say "Enough!" with substance abusers, but I hope you all will have compassion and try to help constructively before you cut them off. I am an alcoholic. Some of it is my fault, and some of it just isn't. That's all there is to it. Do you have a drug addict sibling? What are you doing about it? Calling them weak and turning your back on them? I hope not.

20. *Peter*

"Peter" (I never knew his real name) was from England and was into rubber. He also liked to switch roles from dominant to submissive. He gave me a single photograph of himself as a memento. I have no idea who took the picture — probably, he set a timer and rushed in front of the camera to pose before the shutter clicked. The photo is getting old and beginning to deteriorate in my old, inexpensive photo album. In the photo I have of him, he is head to foot covered in a black rubber costume, fairly tight, with a full head helmet and only two little holes for the eyes and one for his nostrils. He also took a few photos of me, all dressed in rubber. These, too, are in my photo album.

I think he said he was married. We met when he answered an ad I had put in a kinky magazine, advertising myself as either a mistress or a model — I don't remember which. I also don't remember when I first met Peter, but it may have been in the late 1970s. We stayed in touch for nearly a decade, until the fancy car company he worked for transferred him from Connecticut back to England. I had no way of reaching Peter. I'd have to wait for him to get in touch with me. I kept a telephone answering service number for years, and also a Post Office box. Peter was a steady client for such a long time, he usually had my home telephone number as well as my straight job telephone number. He'd usually call about a week before he wanted to see me, and he often visited me in my home, or the apartment I sometimes had access to in my building.

My fee was always the same with him — $100. No set time limits or rules. He usually wanted to have sexual intercourse, but since we were both by the end of each session completely clad in rubber, it wasn't like having sex at all. (When you're head to toe in rubber, it's definitely safe sex!) I found the sessions pretty weird and they did little for me sexually, but Peter was pleasant company and there was always that $100 bill when we were finished. He was on the tall side, good looking, and had a very cultured British accent. He said that over in England, he was a member of a rubber club and they used to have parties, dress up, and engage in sexual intercourse which, as I've just mentioned, has got to be the safest sex on Earth, since there is absolutely no actual direct contact with one's partner when one is completely rubber-clad. He liked both to be spanked and to give a spanking, and he put me in bondage and would allow himself to be tied up, too. He had a huge collection of rubber attire, and it was the expensive, very thick kind. He took very good care of it all, cleaning it in a shower and hanging it to dry, dusting it with powder, then carefully folding it, hiding his large collection in the trunk of his car. (I've had many married clients who've hid their "toys" in their car trunks.)

I don't remember how many times I saw Peter over the years, but it was often. A few times, he even came to see me in whorehouses I was working in, paying the full price, when I was too busy to entertain him at home, or if I had a boyfriend or husband there and couldn't entertain at all. Up until my current (third) marriage, I've never been honest with my spouses or partners about my freelance trick-turning. Usually my partners weren't into kinky stuff, and wouldn't have approved. Also, sneaking around gave the encounters added spice. A titillation factor. One of the last times I saw Peter was the best. This must have been somewhere around 1986 or so. I was working as the research assistant for the junk bond analyst in a big brokerage firm in New York. Right across the street from the tall office tower in which I worked was a famous New York hotel. This hotel, like many others in New York, engaged in the potentially sleazy practice of having "day rates" Ostensibly, you rent a nice hotel room from 9 a.m. to 5 p.m. because you are just passing through town on a business trip and need a place to sleep for a few hours and to take a shower in. Of course, this makes a perfect arrangement for a sexual rendezvous. The hotel didn't advertise their day-rates, but if you inquired discretely, they would hem and haw for a moment or two, then quote you a price — usually a very reasonable one.

I urged Peter to get a room at this hotel on a certain date. I arranged to take a long lunch break. He called me at my office desk and told me he was right across the street in a room, waiting for me. When lunch time came, I reminded my boss I was taking a long break that day, then hurried over to the hotel and into the rubber-clad arms of Peter. He had a bottle of good whiskey and fresh ice and glasses. I hugged him, and we chatted excitedly while I undressed and took sips of whiskey. I smoked pot in those days, so we probably shared a joint. He was already partially dressed in rubber stockings and long rubber gloves. I pulled on a strange rubber skirt which exposed the cheeks of my ass, and put on long rubber gloves and a heavy rubber cape. We took turns spanking each other, taking breaks to chat, sip and puff and enjoy the sensation of tingling butt-flesh from the slaps. Every few minutes, we'd add another item of rubber attire to our outfits from his seemingly bottomless rubber-filled suitcase. My body temperature began to rise, and I started to sweat. The marijuana and unfamiliar hotel room made me feel nervous and weird. Peter continued to embrace me. Finally, he was completely covered in rubber. His suit had a special section to hold his erect penis. He was fairly well endowed, and I saw that he was very sexually aroused. At this point, we lay down on the hotel bed, hugging each other and feeling one another up. Through his tiny nostril openings, I could hear he was breathing harder and heavier. His movements became jerky. He was tremendously excited. He shoved me gently onto my back, and spread my legs apart. The spankings I'd received had lubricated my pussy, so he was able to insert his rubber-encased penis easily into my cunt. In he went, all the way to the balls. By this time, he was puffing and breathing very heavily indeed. He lay on top of me with all his weight, pinning me down, and began to kiss me passionately, although I could really feel nothing because of that full rubber hood he was wearing. (It was impossible to feel his lips when he kissed me — he was all covered up in rubber.) He began the act of sexual intercourse, missionary position, and his strokes increased in tempo. After about five minutes, he arched his back and let out a wail as he ejaculated within his special rubber pants. He collapsed on top of me, breathing hard. Several minutes passed by. Finally, he gathered himself up and pulled out. I looked down and saw that the exterior of the rubber penile pocket was covered with my vaginal lube. "That was great!" he said. "Was it good for you?" I assured him it was (I hadn't had an orgasm but I did get sort of a weird thrill from the encounter), and we both got up and carefully removed our rubber clothing. We took showers, and I dried myself, got dressed back into my work clothes, and finished my whiskey. I collected my $100, thanked him, and made it back to my desk just two hours after I'd departed for my "long lunch" Peter stayed in the room, supposedly to clean and fold his rubber clothing, but for all I know, he stayed there all afternoon and had another woman visit him there!

Of course, we became very friendly over the years we knew each other. He often asked me to introduce him to some of my girlfriends. I had no objection to sharing him with someone else, but knew very few people who would be into his scene. Finally, I met a dominatrix who went by the name Magenta. She was Australian and dreamed of being a singer in a band. During slow times at the kinky whorehouse we both worked in, she'd go into "her" room and play tapes of David Bowie and sing along with him at the top of her lungs. Her voice was pretty good, but not as good as her looks, which were smashing. She was young and pretty, and liked to pose in front of mirrors. I had a feeling she and Peter would get along well. The next time Peter called me, I encouraged him to book an hourlong session with me at the kinky whorehouse on a day when Magenta would be working. He would pay an additional fee, and for part of the session, she would join in with us. Of course, he had to spend a lot more than his usual fee of $100 whenever he saw me in a whorehouse, but this seemed to me to be the most practical way of getting him to meet Magenta.

After Peter was rubber-clad and was tied spread-eagle to a bed (with a rubber sheet on it, of course), I went and fetched Magenta. Their eyes met, locked, and lit up. I was a kinky matchmaker! Magenta and I fondled Peter's rubber-encased penis, then untied him and turned him over and took turns spanking and whipping him. Then we stopped, and Peter sat up and showed Magenta some of the rubber clothing he'd brought along. She admired it tremendously, and tried on a couple of items while we both watched her. She agreed to see Peter again, on her own, and gave him her private telephone number.

I never minded referring one of my clients, private or professional, to a lady I thought they'd hit it off with. I'm not the jealous or possessive type with tricks. That's not realistic. A relationship with a trick is very, very seldom a "real" relationship. I've known a lot of hookers over the years who'd try to snare eligible clients, get involved with them personally, and establish a "real" relationship. I'm not saying this has never come to be — it has — but it is extremely rare. Personally, I feel that a smart man would do well to marry a good whore and set her straight. There's an old saying, "A whore's love is the best love of all."

About a month later, in January 1984, I "retired" from the kinky whorehouse and began attending graduate school at night. I worked all day at a straight job as a secretary in an investment banking house, so had no more time for prostitution as well as a M.B.A. program. Anyway, I had a funny feeling the kinky whorehouse was going to get busted. Sure enough, right after I retired, a very bad bust went down there. Peter told me what Magenta had told him about it. Apparently, a large number of New York City cops surrounded the building, which was on Avenue of the Americas in the 20s, and came charging in, trapping all the girls and their clients. Magenta was in a very bad situation. Since she wasn't an American citizen, and was probably in New York without permission to stay, the police interrogated her and berated her and threatened to arrest her, imprison her for a time, and then deport her back to Australia. She was, of course, terribly frightened. The police also threatened to report her to the Australian authorities, who'd in turn contact her family and tell them exactly what she'd been doing in New York and why she'd been deported. First chance she got, Magenta fled New York, leaving everything behind. She went to live in London.

Peter said he had a phone number for her and they stayed in

touch for awhile. He was really crazy about her and wanted to set her up in England as one of his mistresses once he was transferred back to work in the U.K. Unfortunately, they lost touch. Peter was very saddened and worried about her. I felt bad about introducing them, but at the same time, I felt glad they had had some good times together because I'd introduced them. Peter said that right after the bust, he met with her and she was so shaken, he ended up just hugging her and talking to her and taking her out for something to eat. It was a very sad situation. She told him her real name was Kay. The last time I saw Peter must have been in the late 1980s. He told me his company was transferring him back to an office in England, so he wouldn't be seeing me anymore. Indeed, I never heard from him again. We reminisced about our nearly ten years of rubber-clad meetings, and I was very sad to see him go, but of course, I knew it had to end some time, anyway. By this point, also, I was well into my second marriage, and my second husband would not have been at all pleased to know I was carrying on with Peter as I was.

We embraced, and I reminded him I planned to keep my Post Office box in New York current for many years, and that he could always reestablish contact and I would do my best to see him again. He was very pleased and thanked me, but I could see it in his eyes that he was really sad to be on his way back to England with no trace of Magenta/Kay to follow up on. That's the risk you take when you introduce people, of course — that they'll like each other more than they like you. But I can't be worried about keeping all my clients under my thumb — as I've said, that's just not realistic. Peter was the only client I had who was into rubber quite so much. Myself, I've never cared for sweating in it, nor for the strange claustrophobic feeling I get when I'm all latex-clad.

I've corresponded for many years with another rubber fancier, an elderly gent out in Arizona, and we even met for lunch one day while he was visiting New York on some business. He was retired, but to keep himself occupied, he had a mail-order rubber business. He sold adult-sized diapers and rubber pants for incontinent patients, rubber bedsheets, and a variety of rubber bibs, gloves, aprons and stockings. A few years ago, I ordered a Queen-size fitted rubber mattress protector from him. He sold it to me at cost, and surprised me with a gift package of a wide selection of rubber clothes. Not thick, expensive stuff like Peter had — John's items were thinner, and most of them were made in Malaysia. They came in delightful bright colors, however. A few weeks ago, my third husband and I took the box out of the closet and went through it. My husband put on a pink rubber skirt and a pink rubber t-shirt, and I wore pink rubber long bloomers and a pink rubber apron. We closed our shutters and lounged around the apartment for several hours, rubber-clad. It was vaguely thrilling, but did little to actually sexually stimulate either of us directly very much, so after we'd both worked up a good sweat, we peeled off the clothes, washed them and hung them to dry, and went to bed for half an hour or so to have some conventional sex. The mood had grown decidedly kinky, however, and my husband talked me into giving him an enema — the first one he'd ever had. A couple of hours later, he was wearing panty hose, lying down in our bathtub, and masturbating while I urinated on him. What a kinky Sunday!

I've never had any luck with suppressing any kinky urges I might get. I have to act upon them, sooner or later, or they grow and disturb me. For years, I tried to get my second husband to whip my buttocks with one of his leather belts. He did it once, then stopped and said it was horrible and begged me never to ask him to do it again. Finally, I got my third husband to use a riding crop on my butt, and in time, the urge for this masochistic play evaporated. I no longer want to do that. It's sort of because I know I can have it any time I want, now — it's no longer forbidden fruit. Also, for years I wanted a male lover to urinate on me, especially in my mouth, and I wanted to be forced to drink the piss. I fantasized about this for years, and always hoped one of my dominant clients in the kinky whorehouses I worked in would want to engage in "water sports", but none ever did. Finally, I got my third husband to give me all the piss I wanted, everywhere: in the mouth, on the tits, in my cunt, and once he even fucked me in the ass and then urinated into it. (I got up and ran to the toilet and didn't quite make it — there was some loose shit on our hallway walls I had to clean up later!) We always keep rubber bedsheets handy, but of course, now that I know I can get my husband to piss on me any time I ask him to, I've nearly entirely lost the urge. Go figure!

21. *Carter Stevens*

I did my first bondage modeling for a guy who called himself Carter Stevens. Since the time that I had left home at the age of 18 and gone away to college, I'd become very interested in looking at erotic photographs with sadomasochistic themes. I didn't know any other females who liked looking at "kinky pictures", so I kept quiet about my interest.

When I moved to New York at the age of 20, I befriended a guy named Tom, who lent me a copy of a 1960s fetish magazine he'd bought in a flea market. It was a full-sized, semi-glossy magazine, about 32 pages long, and featured pictures of women wearing very high heels, leather catsuits and underwear, and strange hairdos and lots of makeup. Spanking and other mild dom/sub games were depicted in the magazine. I nearly wore out the pages before I returned the magazine to Tom. The fetishistic images had such an intense impact on me, I spent hours recreating them by doing pen-and-ink drawings of them. I was doing a Xeroxed 'zine at the time called MODERN GIRLZ, and I filled it with my own artwork, and little clippings I'd found here and there of erotic, fetishistic images.

After I moved to Manhattan, I discovered BIZARRE magazine and the cartoons, photographs and writings of John Willie. I hung a "John Willie Bondage Calendar" in the roach-infested kitchen I shared with Paul Martin from 1978-79. I wanted to pose for pictures — kinky pictures — but had no idea how to get set up doing that. Around June of 1978, just after my 21st birthday, I saw an ad in the VILLAGE VOICE asking for models and actresses. There was a telephone number. I called, and was given an address in Chelsea, in the West 20s. It was the studio of Carter Stevens. I wanted to make an impression, so I dressed all in pink. Pink dress, pink underwear, pink stockings, a pink handbag, pink gloves, and I carried a copy of my 'zine, BIKINI GIRL, which was always pink.

The waiting room seemed normal enough, though most of the magazines on the coffee table were adult in nature. A couple of busy-looking secretaries worked at desks, and the phones rang often. Shortly, a man came out and introduced himself as Carter Stevens. He took me to the back of his ground floor loft, which he had converted into a living area. He explained to me that he was a pornographer, and asked me bluntly why I wanted to make "fuck films." I was so surprised by his directness, I mumbled something about earning some extra money. "Forget it," he told me immediately. "There's no money in porn. Don't do it if you need money. There are other more lucrative jobs in the sex industry."

"But I want to," I insisted. We talked for quite awhile. One of the things he told me that I remember most clearly was not to get involved in doing porn unless I was absolutely prepared to have my friends and family "back home" find out about it.

"They'll know right away," said Carter. I told him I didn't care what my family thought about my activities — I still wanted to work in the business of erotica.

Carter talked a little about himself. He was still young, but his hair was thinning. He was fairly tall, but fireplug stocky. Still, he had a wonderful, friendly smile and was very relaxed. He put me at ease right away. He explained that the entire ground floor loft we were in was where he lived and was also the headquarters for his pornographic film business. He told me he did some photographic work for men's magazines and could put me in touch with kinky magazine publishers who needed female models to pose as dominants and submissives. He gave me a couple of telephone numbers to call, and I did get work from some of the people he referred me to.

Carter (which was not, of course, his real name) told me he had been married and had a child, but one day, he'd decided he didn't want to be a grown up anymore, had gotten a divorce, had moved to Manhattan, and had struck out to be a porn king. (Later, he married a second time and had a second child.) Soon, he was making his own full-length, 35mm porn films in the 1970s, when the industry was rapidly growing. His films had a thrown-together look, because he usually shot everything indoors in his Chelsea studio. There are very few outdoors shots or location shots in the porn movies of Carter Stevens. He also tended to use cheap sets and costumes, and second-string actors and actresses. What his films lacked in artistic merit, they made up for with hardcore pornographic action. His movies also usually had a sense of humor about them.

We talked for a long time, and he asked me if I was interested in doing "loops." These were shot on 16mm film (I think) and were about ten minutes long — until the film ran out. These short movies would then be run in peep shows. They were fairly easy work, he told me, and paid $50 cash on the spot for each loop done. I didn't like the idea of it, so declined. Carter seemed truly disappointed. "What would you really like to do?" he asked me.

"Still modeling," I told him. "Kinky stuff. Like, me tied up and stuff like that." Carter seemed very interested.

"Have you ever done that type of work before?"

"No," I replied, "but it interests me even more than porn movies. I like to look at non-moving photographic images — kinky, sexy ones."

"Then you should be a bondage model," he said.

"Okay," I replied.

"I'll make you the next Bettie Page!" he exclaimed, rubbing his hands excitedly.

"Who's that?" I asked. He just stared at me. He couldn't believe that at my age (21) and with a clear interest in erotic photography, I didn't know who the great Bettie Page was! I also knew nothing, at this time, of the work of Irving Klaw.

"Bettie Page was a bondage model," Carter told me. "A very good one. Possibly the greatest."

"Then I want to be the next Bettie Page," I said.

At one point, I was lying on my back on Carter's big platform bed in the back of his studio. I was naked, and he had fastened leather cuffs to my wrists and ankles. Each cuff had a chain on it, attached to rings at the four corners of the bed. My legs were wide apart, and he was fucking me. He was staring down at me. Shyly, I turned my head to one side. "Why are you looking away?" he asked, pulling my head so I was facing him. Again, I shyly turned my head to the side. Heterosexual sex was all still pretty new to me, and I was genuinely bashful. "You like being a slave, don't you?" he said to me. Not knowing what to do or say, I nodded. "Oh, yeah, you like it, you little slut," he said to me, or words to that effect. Oddly, I found submitting to him strangely satisfying. I was tied down — there weren't many options for me to squirm around or have an equal part in the sex act. Something about the submissive role appealed to me a lot. I guess at that time in my life, it was just easier to submit. Less complicated. But beyond that, I got an odd sexual thrill from it all.

Over the next few months, I visited Carter in his ground floor loft fairly often. He shot several rolls of photographic film of me in suspension. The background for the pictures was a dungeon setting. I had an allergic reaction to all the hay scattered around on the floor, and got a sinus infection. He did a one-shot glossy magazine (it was called "Chained") and most of the pictures were of me. I was also the centerfold, hanging there, cuffed, suspended by chains. Carter liked chains a lot. (Apparently, "Chained" is being published again.) The modeling work didn't pay too much, and after awhile, he stopped photographing me. "The porn market is really soft right now," he explained. (He later admitted there were problems going on in his personal life, and he just wasn't paying much attention to marketing his material at that point in time.) I continued to decline to do loops. At summer's end, he was doing a full-length porn movie called "Double Your Pleasure," which starred the Sloan twins. He offered me the part of Gloria, the lazy secretary whose boss spanks her. The pay was $150 for a full day's work, $75 for a half day's work.

We started preparing in the late afternoon or early evening. A kindly black fag who claimed to have worked for Fellini did my makeup and hair. He was very good. I stared back at myself in the brightly lit mirror — I had been transformed. He had completely changed my appearance with his makeup job. I didn't have a good figure in those days. Come to think of it, I've never had a good figure. My breasts were nearly nonexistent. My best features were my clear skin, my long dark blonde hair, my big eyes and youthful appearance.

I was introduced to my sex partner for our scene. I think his name was David. He was very good looking. I asked him if he had any drugs. He looked alarmed, then hustled me into one of the bathrooms. "Don't say things like that out loud!" he said, then turned me on to a little coke. I was pretty nervous. My part called for only a few lines. Wardrobe had been unable to provide me with anything nice to wear for my big moment on the porn screen, so I wore the pink dress and some of my own lingerie from home. David played my boss. He asked me if I had finished my work for the day, and when I said I hadn't, he told me I'd have to be punished, to which I happily agreed. A desk was cleared, and I was strapped to it somehow. David held my legs up in the air and fucked me.

By now, it was around 4 in the morning. The studio was brightly lit, and there were crew members everywhere behind the whirring cameras. Occasionally, action would stop and still photographers would snap away. These photos would appear in men's magazines, and I would receive no extra pay for them. (Carter says he didn't, either.) I think our scene took about half an hour to shoot. When it was all over, I changed and gathered up my things and took a cab back to the apartment on East 10th Street I shared with Paul Martin. The sun had come up, but it was still very early. I had a check for $150 in my bag — enough to buy those skintight leather jeans I had been craving all summer. I was crashing severely from the coke comedown, and was also in a state of shock from just having done a porn scene in a feature film. (The reality of it all didn't really start to hit me until just after the actual shooting ended! I was really a babe in the woods.)

I took a cab home in the early morning light to my shared East Village apartment. There were roaches crawling all over the dishes in the sink. Paul, my roomie, had left me a nasty note about not doing my fair share of the housework, and called me a slob. I held the note, and started to cry. Paul woke up in the other room, got up off his mattress on the floor, and came over to give me a hug. My tears really shook him. He apologized again and again for the nasty note. "I didn't mean to upset you so much," he said. For a long time, we just stood there, holding each other. I wanted to tell Paul I had just done something really stupid — done a porn scene in a 35mm fuck film — but soon my thoughts were on cooking up our favorite breakfast: fried potatoes, onions, eggs, lots of ketchup on the side. Paul had a special little espresso pot and made good coffee. I decided not to tell him where I'd been all night.

Later that same day, I went uptown, near the shoe store where I worked full-time, and bought the leather jeans. Knowing I would wear them in the store and refer customers to the leather shop, the sales help in the leather shop sold me those jeans with no sales tax due. Those sexy leather jeans had no lining and really did fit like a second skin. I stood for hours in front of an old full-length mirror in the buggy kitchen I shared with Paul, changing sweaters and turning around and around, admiring how I looked in those jeans.

As I write this, I feel sick at the memory of my foolishness. What on earth was so damned important about a pair of tight leather jeans that I had to appear in a porn movie to get them? I guess I would feel more ashamed about the whole thing if the film had been a huge success, but instead, the porn movie was a flop and faded immediately into porn obscurity. No one has ever come up to me and said, "I remember you from 'Double Your Pleasure!'" I have a copy of the movie on videotape, and sometimes look at my scene, which was about ten minutes long, total, after editing. I don't recognize myself. Apparently, no one else I know has, either. I continued to stay in touch with Carter Stevens for a long time.

We weren't great friends or anything, but he was a nice man. Nicest pornographer I've ever known!

I got quite a bit of modeling work from some people he referred me to. One day I turned on the TV news and there was Carter, being led in handcuffs out the front door of his porn studio/loft. He was accused of using an underage female in one of his projects. He was eventually acquitted, but not until his legal defense took every last dollar he had. I remember talking to him about it, when it was all over, and he said he had probably just gotten too big for his britches — an annoyance to the City of New York — and they put him in jail just long enough to wipe him out financially. He moved to another loft and continued to work in porn, but things were never the same for him.

Carter's second marriage, which was to a stripper, failed, and he moved away from New York, out to the country, where he published an adult tabloid featuring S/M. Of course, there was a personal ad section. For quite a few years, I ran ads in his publication. I was doing this as late as 1992. I got hundreds of letters. Many of them were truly strange, but most of them were from lonely males who seemed nice enough.

One guy, a student at NYU, sent me a very interesting letter, and I called him and we agreed to meet at a bar near the campus. I showed up on time and sat up front, sipping a whiskey. A youngish guy came in, looked at me, and turned and walked out. Guess I wasn't his fantasy-come-true. Or maybe I was, and he couldn't handle it.

The last time I ran an ad in Carter's publication, I got about 150 letters. I made a date with the first one I opened and met the guy — who is "Don", in chapter 17 — at Fanelli's bar in SoHo. We talked for a couple of hours over numerous drinks, and decided to meet again in his nearby studio apartment as soon as my dose of the flu cleared up. Don turned out to be a wonderful person and an excellent slave, and we are still in touch.

But how long will my life be? How long before I find out I am HIV positive, or that the damage I have done to my liver with years of heavy drinking is finally going to kill me? What kind of a life do I have left, and why did I do all the self-destructive things I did in my youth? Of course, I don't have the answers. But the questions cause me to lose a lot of sleep. I don't know where Carter is or what he's up to these days. Except for two slaves, Angelo and Don, I've fallen out of touch with almost everyone I knew from the porn and S/M world I was so much a part of in New York in the '70s and '80s. Many of the people I knew disappeared. Of course, quite a few of them are dead.

22. *Substance Abuse*

At this writing, I am 41 years old. I am overweight and in poor health. I'm unemployed. After my second marriage in New York failed, it finally happened — I took an interest in hard drugs. I'd always been so proud that I only smoked marijuana and drank alcohol, although, in fact, I had nothing to be proud of — I abused pot and booze to a staggering excess. I got drunk and stoned on lunch hours at my straight jobs; hence, my very checkered C.V. I always blamed my employers for their unfairness whenever I was fired. I never placed the blame on myself and my addictions. I've spent most of my so-called "adult" life blaming others for everything.

Now, I have had a lot of bad stuff happen to me, it's true. Some of my misfortunes have been due to the wickedness of others, and some have been due to chance. Bad luck. But a lot of the bad things I've experienced, I brought upon myself entirely. I see that so clearly now. And it's too late. I'm dying of alcoholism. A lot of my problems have existed because I have an enormous streak of Protestant Work Ethic in me — or some such fucking thing. I am not sure how to label it. I've never been on public assistance, except for getting Food Stamps a few times. I've always worked, either at straight jobs or at kinky ones, to earn money to take care of myself. And take care of myself I have — in my own messed-up fashion.

I left my parents' home when I was 18. By my second year of college, I was mostly self-supporting, and since the time I moved to New York at age 20, I've been on my own completely. I guess I should feel proud that I financed my own education and have a Bachelor degree and a Master degree. I did a lot of work as a temporary legal secretary to pay for my M.B.A. degree. Long days, tedious tasks, hard-to-please attorneys, spiteful co-workers who feared they'd be let go and "the temp" would take their spots. It was extremely difficult work. Again, I guess I should feel proud of my accomplishments, but everything in my mind is clouded by my thousands upon thousands of regrets, large and small. I used to think I was happy, was living an action-packed, fairly enviable life, that my artistic projects were valid, that I had lots and lots of friends. I was dead wrong on most counts. True, I lived the crazy New York life nearly to the fullest for almost 20 years, but I can look back on it now and see it was just a flurry of mad, mindless activity, to conceal how deeply fearful and unhappy I really was.

As I write this, I am suffering from all the effects of full-blown alcoholism, which will probably kill me soon. I was on psych meds for the past couple of years, after spending five days in a mental hospital. I suffer from depression. Since about the age of 16, I have tried to medicate myself with alcohol. I smoked a lot of pot in New York. Currently, I've managed to get away from mari-juana, but feel intense shame at the thousands and thousands of dollars I've wasted on it. Alcohol is a whole 'nuther dreary ball of wax. In Europe, I cannot afford to buy hard liquor very often, so I've become a wino. Left to my own devices, I will drink two to four bottles of wine a day. And start very early in the morning — such as 7:00 a.m.

A few months ago, the trembling in my hands each morning began, and most of this year, I've had vomiting spells at the beginning of each day. I never used to vomit. Even with an empty stomach, I retch most mornings and have to sit for about an hour before my stomach settles down. Needless to say, it is often quite difficult to eat. My abdomen has grown very large, and my liver very tender to the touch. I am drinking myself to death. Since I get temporary secretarial work from time to time, I drink much, much less when I have to get up in the morning and go to an office somewhere. I still can't entirely give up the bottle. I'm in danger. Recently, I abruptly stopped taking the psych meds I was on for depression. I didn't tell my shrink until two weeks later. (I see him basically just as a pill-pusher, anyway. He just makes faces, asks to see copies of my writing, writes prescriptions, and tells me to see him again in a week.)

As soon as I decided to simply stop taking all the psych meds, I had severe, extremely bizarre nightmares. Then, over the course of the next few weeks, my face lost some of its puffiness. I don't miss the heavy medication — such as Haldol — at all, but still need to take a sleeping pill to get to sleep sometimes — half a pill when I go to bed, and the other half four hours later, when the

first half wears off and I am suddenly wide awake. I sleep extremely poorly and am troubled by anxiety dreams and night sweats. A
few weeks ago, I was so sick and hung over from alcoholism, I literally could not get up from the mattress anymore. I hadn't the
strength to cook myself anything to eat. Each night, I'd get chills
and the mattress would be damp with my perspiration. Now, I am
able to make it through some days without a drink at all, but generally, I have two or three glasses of wine. My face immediately gets
red and hot, and an hour later, I feel nauseated and shaky. My
body is no longer able to process and digest alcohol. I've reached
the end of the trail. I can't help but feel that somehow, God is pun-
ishing me for my past pride.

I watched so many friends fall victim to drug addictions in
New York, or lose the battle with the bottle. I gossiped about
them, looked down my nose at them. Sometimes, I'd try to say
something like, "You should get into rehab or something," but I
don't recall ever going out of my way to really DO anything for
anyone. Maybe because my first husband was a heroin addict and
I learned the hard way never to trust a junkie, I tended to look
upon addicted persons without much pity Sometimes, I'd notice I
hadn't seen so-and-so in the clubs for a long time, and I'd ask
around after them and be told they'd had to pack up, leave New
York, and move back in with their families to get away from the
temptation of easily available drugs in the big, bad city. "That's too
bad," I can hear myself say. Then, I'd change the subject and go to
the bar for another round of drinks. THAT couldn't happen to

ME. I was too strong. I'd never have to leave New York to get away from my addictions. How wrong I was.

In January, 1994, after I had left my second husband and moved back into a rent-stabilized apartment in Brooklyn I'd sub-let and regained, the shame and sadness over my divorce, com-bined with the threatening telephone calls from my ex, who usual-ly demanded money (and usually got it) drove me to drink my vodka straight and count my sleeping pills, ready to swallow them all and do away with myself. As always, I smoked pot to give myself a lift. At this time, however, I started to frequent Washington Square Park, where it was extremely easy to buy drugs. I learned to hand roll my own tobacco cigarettes, and to finely chop up rocks of crack cocaine and mix them in — a "dirty ciga-rette" Crack took away all my anxiety and filled me with an intense calm. It eliminated all physical pain. I couldn't eat when I was on crack — I wasn't hungry. I became extremely passive, just lying back on the mattress, staring at the ceiling. I asked around for cocaine, and found some connections. Very easily.

By the middle of 1994, I was unemployed (again!) and tak-ing steps to leave New York forever. My divorce had become final. I painstakingly had all my personal i.d. papers converted back to my maiden name. I had fallen in love again, and planned to escape to a new life in Europe. And I did. But my alcoholism immigrat-ed with me. I guess there's no reason for me to conceal where I live now: I live in Saint-Denis, a suburb of Paris, France. The bars open very early. Most people are there for coffee, but no one stares if you ask for a drink of alcohol at 8 in the morning. The wine is excellent, of course, and if you look carefully, you can find a decent enough bottle for under $2. With all the stresses of having to adapt to a new country, learn a new language, secure my immigration status, get married (for the third time), find a place to live, and find employment, I quickly developed a massive wine habit.

I've always wanted the opportunity to write a book about my crazy years in New York, bondage modeling and doing other wild things. Now that the opportunity has presented itself and I can sit and type and tell you all about it, I feel overwhelmed by the task, and sickened by my memories. Turning 40 probably has a lot to do with it — I realize my life is probably more than half over. Funny: I used to look forward to old age. Now, I fear it. I don't fear death, I just fear the decline in health and vigor which is to come. I fear the death of my husband, and being alone in this strange country. I do speak French, but not very well. I was 37 years old when I immigrated. Probably too old for such a drastic change. If you're thinking of immigrating, I advise against it. A lot of the people I knew in New York were just fairweather friends, but those who've stayed in touch and have even come to visit me in Europe are half a world away. I'm intensely lonely. I lead a very quiet life — too quiet.

The other day, I went to the center of town to visit the bank and to buy some vegetables in the open-air market. It was a bleak, snowy day. I stood shivering, waiting for the bus, and thought to myself: Lisa, you're not enjoying this. Paris is an interesting, romantic place to visit, but not a very nice place to live. The air is very dirty. True, the streets are cleaned often, but that doesn't do much good — people let their dogs shit all over the place. Everything here seems gray. The climate is uncomfortable. Winters are depressing, summers unbearably hot — and almost no place is air conditioned. Unemployment is high, salaries tend to be low. The cost of living is terrifying, taxation crushing. The work days are long. Commutes are also long, despite a fairly extensive public transportation system. To fulfill the obligations of my current temp job, I get up at 6, leave the apartment at 7:45 a.m. to get to work by 9:00, work until 6:00 p.m. or later, get home around 7:30 or 8:00 at night, cook a small, uninteresting meal for myself and my husband, take a sleeping pill, and try to be unconscious before 10.

Families tend to be close in France, so I usually have to give up a big part of my weekend to visit with my in-laws, have an intolerably long, high-fat lunch with them and too much alcohol, only to go home and rush to shop (mostly for wine) before the stores close. There's laundry to do, housework, and suddenly, it's Sunday night. Have to get to bed early to get up for work Monday morning. We never go out — it's too expensive.

Many French people smoke and drink too much. Almost everyone here looks at least ten years older than they really are. More people suffer from depression in Paris than almost any place else on Earth. (Beirut is the winner.) During the long periods of time between unemployment, I do a lot of sitting, staring out the window at a tall apartment building across the street from my own tall apartment building, and I read — almost one book every two days. I listen to the BBC on the radio. I don't have a television — French TV is terrible, anyway. And, of course, there's a television tax. Yes, you read that right. Lower tax if your TV is black and white, higher tax if your TV is color. There is a "habitation tax", which is a tax you pay for having a roof over your head. Whether you own or rent your abode, you pay the habitation tax. And the French just put up with this shit!

Just about the only bright spot in my life is my husband. He's ten years younger than I am, French, well read, quick to joke, and he likes to cross-dress. I'm married to a young French transvestite. Sometimes it's kind of like having a girlfriend. Am I regressing to my lesbian days? He works in the computer industry, is dreadfully underpaid and unappreciated by his employer, and he likes to experiment sexually. Almost anything goes! A year or so ago I let him persuade me to submit to anal sex — something I'm not interested in much at all. After sodomizing me for half and hour or so, he realized he had to pee. He just went ahead and urinated in my ass. I didn't realize what he had done until he pulled out — shit and piss dribbling uncontrollably out of my butt! I ran for the toilet. "Why did you do that?" I gasped, laughing in spite of myself. "I don't know," he replied. There was shit on the hallway walls. We both giggled and wiped it up, then changed the bedding together. (One of our wedding presents to ourselves was a rubber mattress protector. We need it!)

I've just reread what I've written in this chapter, and it seems out of place with the rest of the chapters so far. But I had to write it. I am deeply ashamed of my alcoholism. I've had more than one doctor here tell me I am not alcoholic, by French standards! Man, the French are a mess. One of these doctors told me that above all, I should not feel ashamed that I drink too much and too often. But he didn't tell me what the fuck I am supposed to feel instead of shame! Pride, perhaps? Yeah, let me go and look in the mirror and check out my rotten complexion once more, then I'll come back and tell you how proud I am of myself. Sheeeesh! I've almost always been an impulsive person of very poor and erratic judgement. I've been certified mentally ill on two continents! The reason I'm ranting about my filthy addiction is because I think a lot of the crazy things I did in the past, such as selling my body, were done because I was either drunk, not in my right mind, or both. I find myself wanting to say, "Don't let this happen to you!" but I spent too many years in the Life, the bizarre life, to know better than to hope I can really do anything to stop anyone from doing self-destructive things. People get weird urges to do weird things. Take it from me.

I am amazed, however, that I've managed to carve out a kind of "cottage industry" for myself as a bondage model for the past 20+ years. Maybe I'm a little bit proud of that. There are thousands of pictures out there of me, tied up and wriggling, eyes wide. Many of the photographers who've hired me recognized me immediately. I am sure a lot of straight co-workers have, too, but they sure as shit weren't going to admit it! Well, it has taken me nearly

I WAS FOR SALE.

a month to write these last few pages. I'm going to stop ruminating about all this crap and move on to the next chapter. Because just the other day, I remembered this guy from Africa who used to visit New York once a year or so...

23. *The White Slaver*

About once a year, Jim's work as an international tax consultant would require him to visit New York, and he'd call my answering service and leave his name and room number. He always stayed at the Hotel Edison — so the answering service would just say to me, "Jim called at three and said he's in 210."

I saw Jim for about twelve years, I estimate. After getting one of his messages, I'd return the call and we'd make a date, then I'd walk over to the West side of Manhattan, smiling when I saw the big poster for "Oh, Calcutta!", the nude musical that seemed to always be playing in a theatre adjacent to the Edison. That huge poster (or maybe it was a painted mural — I don't remember) was like an old friend to me, representing some kinky fun I'd have and a hundred dollar bill I'd soon have in my hand.

I'd make it a point to show up for my appointments with Jim early, so I could sit in the hotel bar for a little while before-hand. This was a totally pointless ritual, since Jim was waiting for me upstairs, knew I am a drinker, and always had a bottle of liquor and fresh ice and drinking glasses on hand, but I loved the bar in the Edison so much, having my pre-Jim cocktail there became a cherished habit. A must-do. I'd waste five dollars or so drinking in that hotel bar, when I could have gone straight up to Jim's room and had drinks for free, but I still went to the hotel bar, anyway. Do you like hotel bars? I do. I guess that's the slut in me. But I guess that's also the lazy lush in me, too — hotel bars are seldom crowded, tend to be clean and comfortable (although overpriced), and there is usually a good bathroom. Hotel bars are often truly "cocktail lounges" — you can really kick back and just tie on a nice little drunk.

One of the other reasons I like drinking in hotel bars is because I like sitting there alone, either at the bar or at a table, and thinking to myself, "I really am a prostitute. Does anyone suspect me? Is anyone going to try to pick me up?" In truth, I don't recall ever being approached by anyone in a hotel bar, though an exception to this might be that cool bar in the Chelsea Hotel on West 23rd Street. I've had some interesting times there. I am not a cigarette smoker (I was addicted from age 18 to age 20, and quitting was so horrible, I never got the habit again) but I do love a nice menthol cigarette while drinking in a hotel bar. Preferably a Benson & Hedges Deluxe Ultra Light Menthol cigarette. I took a liking to that brand when the manufacturer mailed me two free packs in 1982. Fortunately, they don't sell that brand where I live now, or I'd almost surely be a smoker again. Cigarettes cost about four dollars a pack in Paris. Very bad habit, smoking in France.

Well, anyway, I'd drink up, pay up, and head for the elevators. The Edison is a huge hotel, usually full of tourists of every stripe. If there was any hotel security watching me on my way to see Jim, I sure didn't spot 'em. Jim always greeted me with a broad grin, and he had a charming British accent. (I don't like British accents much, but his was an African colonial variety and sounded absolutely terrific.) We'd always sit for up to half an hour in the rather uncomfortable chairs provided in the hotel room, at a little table with the liquor bottle and ice bucket and glasses set up on it, and catch up on each others' lives. He wasn't terribly old, but as time wore on, his health began to fail, and I think he's dead now, so I'm writing about him in the past tense. Last time I saw him, he'd had a nasty experience during a stopover in London — a gall bladder attack, or something — bad enough that he was hospitalized there for several days, to have the offending organ taken out. Didn't sound promising to me. I figured this would be my last fling with ol' Jim boy, and sure enough, I never saw him again, though I've carefully kept in place for 20+ years now a means for all clients who really want to see me to track me down, wherever I may be. (Nyah, nyah, I'm not going to tell you what it is!)

So, Jim would usually show me pictures of his family back there in Africa. With each passing year, I watched his kids get taller in the snapshots he'd show me. In some of the pictures, the family posed with their black domestic workers. White supremacy was on its way out in his particular country, but his family had had the same employees for years and years, and everyone seemed to get along just fine. Although maybe those smiling black domestics were really thinking, "God, I can't wait to waste these honkeys." I dunno. In one of the pictures, he showed me his kids sitting on and posing around a pet donkey Jim had bought them to play with and ride. The donkey lived in their garden. That pet donkey captured my fancy, so I always asked after the donkey, knowing full well it hadn't lived long. For some odd reason, I enjoyed seeing Jim's rather wistful smile as he sighed and said, "Oh, well, that donkey, he just didn't make it."

Now that I think of it, I think Jim only showed me a picture of his wife once — maybe. I think the pictures were always of the kids, or the house, or the gardens. Of course I wondered why he didn't talk much about his wife, but I sure as hell didn't press the matter. My clients would either yak about their wives non-stop, or they'd fall mum on the subject. Seldom was there anything in between. The wives were either loved or hated, but for whatever reasons, were not involved with hubby's penchant for hiring bondage models. After the drinks and chat, Jim would usually ask me the same question, year after year: "You're a happy person, aren't you?"

"Yes," I always answered him, usually fully believing myself at the time.

"That's terrific," he'd mutter, smiling, looking away and kind of shaking his head. It seemed hard for him to believe a bondage model could be a reasonably normal and fairly happy person. In retrospect, of course, I realize I was neither normal nor happy at all. But like all good girls, I told the trick just what he wanted to hear. Never rile a trick. He'll either never see you again, or worse, he'll drop a dime on you. No, come to think of it, worse still, he might maim or kill you or something. Obviously, I didn't think about that much, while I was for sale. What a crap shoot!

Jim's fantasy was being a white slaver. I don't think that's a very amusing fantasy these days, but back when I was seeing Jim, his scene entertained me. His camera was loaded and ready. I don't remember if it was a Polaroid or not — I think it was some type of instamatic. Jim took lots and lots of pictures of me during our sessions, but unlike most of my other customers, never mailed me copies of the photos, as he was fairly certain his mail was being monitored, due to the tense political situation in his country. He gave me a P.O. Box address where I could write to him in a neighboring country in Africa that he visited often on business, and I sent him my one-shot bondage magazine, PENANCE AND PUNISHMENT, and sure enough, he never received it.

I don't own copies of any of the pictures he took of me. Sometimes, he'd want me naked, sometimes, half-dressed. He'd use neckties and bind my wrists over my head. Sometimes on the rod in the hotel room closet, sometimes on the shower head in the bathroom... he'd either close the closet door or the bathroom door, depending on the room arrangement for that visit, and his mood, I suppose, and I'd have to pretend to sort of hang there for a few minutes in the dark. Of course, I couldn't really put my body weight on the closet rod or the shower head, or it would have broken. Then, he'd jubilantly throw open the door, snap on a light, and declare, "So, you're coming around, are you?" And I'd have to pretend to be gaining consciousness from some sort of drugged state. He'd slap me around a little, and then feel me up, tweaking my breasts, leering, possibly jerking off a little. "Yes, I've bought you," he'd mutter, by now fully caught up in the scene, "and I'm going to be the first one to have you!"

"Where am I?" I'd moan.

"That doesn't matter," he'd reply. "You're my prisoner. I bought you in a slave auction and I'm in the process of delivering you to another owner who'll give me good money for you. But, in the meantime, I'm going to be the first one to have you!" As I moaned, resisted, and put up a very, very feeble fight, he'd loosen the neckties and lead me to the bed, where he'd sort of tie me up again, but often I'd just pretend to be tied one way or another. "Nice, young body," he'd say softly, feeling me all over, and I'd pretend to recoil from his touch and to panic and try to talk my way out of the "situation."

"Please, whatever you do to me, don't rape me!" I'd beg him. "My family has money! They'll pay to get me back! But I'm only 16 and I've had a decent upbringing and I must stay a virgin until I marry!"

"Hahhah!" he'd chuckle, at this point usually squeezing my breasts hard enough to produce bruises that might last a week or so. I didn't really care. Getting bruised was part of the deal, and I learned how to avoid the scrutiny of husbands and lovers by taking fluffy bubble baths and slipping into long, silky robes before they could see the bruises. And if they ever did see me, I'd simply say, "I bruise easily," which is true.

Jim often had on hand "torture devices", innocuous things such as plastic forks or a candle he'd light and drip wax on my chest. I was to pretend these were needles, knives or branding irons, and to withdraw and recoil from them in feigned intense pain. From my position, flat on my back on a hotel bed, I couldn't see if he was hard or not, but I think he generally wasn't. He was getting on in years. I'd pretend to bargain with him. My family would pay any price he demanded to have me safely returned home, my precious virginity intact. He'd only laugh and say, "No, no, my dear, too late. You shouldn't have been in such-and-such a place and been talking with strangers" (or some such thing), "and now, here you are, my captive. Oh, yes, I'm going to get a fine price for you!" My playacting must have been lamentable, as I'd toss my head from side to side, moan, pretend to struggle against nonexistent (usually) bonds, and beg and beg for my release and for my precious virginity. He'd then spread my legs and pretend to examine my vulva. "Definitely still a virgin," he'd chuckle. "Oh, yes, I'll get a fine price for you, my dear."

It was kind of hard to keep in the spirit of things, as he'd pause fairly often to take a photograph of me. One nice thing about Jim, however, was that often he'd show me, along with the snaps of his family, snaps of nice call-girls he'd tied up in foreign cities. He showed me a picture of a pretty brunette he'd recently "enslaved" in London. "Fine girl, happily married, job, really got into the spirit of things. Adorable!" he chanted, as I peered at a photograph of a nice-looking lingerie-clad young woman in some distant hotel room. I've always been interested in seeing pictures of other bondage models. So, after about 30 minutes of this nonsense, Jim would be hard and would put on a condom and would gloat, "Now, now, I'm going to HAVE you!" and then I'd have to thrash about (but not too much!) and not make so much noise as to bring on the hotel security staff, and he'd somehow get his pecker into me and I'd say stuff like, "Oh, my God, please kill me now, I'm no longer a virgin, I can't believe you're raping me," and he'd go into this litany, like, "Yes, yes, you're being raped my dear, so sorry old girl," and blessedly, he'd soon begin to groan and then let out quite a loud scream as he shot his load into the scumbag! (My current husband also screams when he squirts — I still find it more than a little disquieting, at times.)

I'd get to thinking, "Oh, please God, don't let him die of a heart attack on me, my fingerprints are on file with the FBI..." and other nice thoughts, which I'd usually manage to cast asunder by focusing on the hundred dollar bill I knew I'd soon receive, plus at least another twenty for my cab fare home to Brooklyn. Invariably, after the session I'd walk to a bank teller machine, make the deposit into my account, and take the subway home, saving the twenty for a nice restaurant lunch the next day, or sometimes, even hot, fresh takeout food for Husband Two, who was waiting for me at home. ...Husband Two stopped fucking me regularly after our first year of marriage. For various reasons, I stuck around for another eight years of this nonsense. One of the things that kept us together so long was he usually didn't ask too many questions about my regular disappearing acts. I could shower after the sessions with Jim if I wanted to, but I don't think I ever did, as my meetings with him were never of the sweat-inducing variety. Relatively easy work, and not terribly disturbing (at the time). And so, I'd dress, maybe have another drink if it hadn't gotten too late, and we'd wish each other well and embrace lightly and off I'd go, walking East toward Sixth Avenue, to the teller machine and the F train.

Jim, whatever happened to you? What inspired your fantasy? Living in Africa, in a country with most privileges given to whites? I guess that's the answer, but still, I wonder. And really, I almost enjoyed the fantasy, myself, which is also pretty weird. In truth, I can think of few things more horrific than finding oneself sold into slavery. I read about slavery in the papers a lot these days. I think there are about six million slaves in the world today. It isn't funny, of course, but what aspect of bondage fantasy is really humorous, anyway? None that I can think of. It's all pretty dark and dreary stuff, isn't it? Even tickling games are thinly veiled acts of aggression and torture. Almost always, over the years, the cash I'd earn from bondage modeling was used almost immediately to pay utility bills, to buy groceries, to go see a dentist... For reasons not at all clear to me, I'd tend to squander my paychecks from straight jobs on restaurant meals, bags of pot, bottles of brand-name liquor, gifts and fripperies. As I mentioned before, some twisted streak in me made me put most of what I earned illicitly into retirement accounts and such — the money I earned on the side was nearly always put to some very serious use. And sadly, during my second divorce, I gave most of my assets and retirement accounts away, to gain some piece of mind and to assuage my guilt and my shame over the failure of that terrible marriage. I never charged much money for private clients. About a hundred dollars was the top. What on Earth possessed me?

24. *Bondage Babies*

Debbie Revenge and I were on an Amtrak train to New England. What year was it? Must have been 1981 or 1982. I still don't understand much about junkies, even though I had been married to one. Debbie was very open with me about her habit. At this particular moment, she needed to crap — it had been days — but no crap was forthcoming. We had fortified ourselves for the trip with munchies, pot, and her favorite straight high, a small bottle of peppermint schnapps.

"Schnapps is the best cheap high," Debbie chanted. I couldn't argue with the price. It was around a dollar twenty five back then. She was so addled, she couldn't remember the name of the Nedick's stand in the train station in Manhattan. "Meet me by that place with the great hot dogs," was all she could say. To date, she is the only native New Yorker I have ever met who couldn't remember the name of fucking Nedick's hot dogs. I don't mean to imply from the gitgo that Debbie was a mess. No. Debbie was right on top. Top of the heap. It was a garbage heap, but she knew it and reveled in it.

She claimed to have been part-owner of a used clothing shop in the East Village on Second Avenue just South of Saint

Mark's Place in the late seventies. The name of the shop was "Revenge", so she was known as "Debbie Revenge." (She acted in at least one porn movie under this moniker, as well.) Everything in the Revenge store was two dollars. Usually the used clothing sold therein needed mending, but I never complained when I made my purchases there. I could put together a cool punk outfit for cheap at the Revenge store, as long as I had access to a needle and black thread to do a little quick repair work on the clothes I bought there. She came from a good family, she said. Doctors. Upper West Side or something. She told me her real family name. I won't repeat it here, but it rhymes with "early" I doubt she is still alive, but her family might not appreciate seeing their name in print.

Debbie was a good whore. True to her word. If she borrowed twenty from you and said you'd have it back in a week or so, she'd make the effort to slap that cash back right in your palm as soon as she could. In her own way, she was very honest and direct. She had the very old-fashioned New York habit of calling her sister whores "girlfriend" I remember well the first of each month in the East Village. The rent was due. There was tension in the air. Mine wasn't usually a high rent, thank God, but it was due nonetheless to your Slumlord and you kind of gazed out the window and saw the eagle fly, as if directly from your pocket out the window and into the atmosphere. To cheer myself on such days, I'd play "House Rent Boogie" by John Lee Hooker. Debbie didn't seem to live anywhere, didn't seem worried by first-of-the-month rent due. She floated.

Johnny Thunders was her boyfriend. They were always having arguments over his drug habit. Since she was a junkie herself, it seemed a little ridiculous to me that she'd nag at him for doing heroin. She'd cry to me, "Lisa, I tell him, `You've got to stop, kids look up to you, you're a rock'n'roll star, you're killing yourself.' And he won't quit." But neither would she. I first met her when we were call girls together. She looked a tad scruffy for the role, but not by far. Overall, she was cute and pretty — she still had her youthful looks. Her kinky blonde dyed hair was usually worn in an upsweep, and she had some cute little sundresses. She was the only junkie I ever knew who didn't fuss about wearing long sleeves. Her arms weren't scarred or marked by the needle, as far as I could see. Maybe she shot heroin in her thigh veins — a lot of whores I knew did that. Or maybe between her toes — I heard people did that, too. I didn't ask her. I didn't want to know. She'd speak frankly to me about her heroin use, and I try not to think about it too much. I've never done heroin — it's just not something I can understand or relate to.

She had nice high cheekbones and her skin wasn't great, but it was very white. As I've said, she still had her youthful good looks, for the most part. No figure to speak of, but put her in black jeans and her red leather biker jacket and she sure looked tough. She got picked often enough when we were straight whores, and apparently kept the tricks happy. But while I was away at art school in Italy over the Summer of 1981, she got heavier into the junk and her friends stopped sheltering her. She took to sleeping in the whorehouse. After she was fired, I asked the Madame, Katherine, what had happened to Debbie, and was told, "She had to go. I got her a week's hotel stay." I tracked down Debbie to get her side of the story.

"Katherine fired you?"

"Yeah, and she had the nerve to buy me a room for a week at the hotel Seton and say, 'There's nothing more I can do for you.' The nerve! I have FRIENDS in this town! I insisted the hotel give me the cash for the room right in my hand and I marched my butt outta there. Fuck her!" Myself, I thought it was rather nice of Katherine to offer such severance to Debbie, who was often late to work cuz she'd o.d.'d, but I kept quiet on this point. In fact, I used a room once to turn a trick later at the Seton, and the room was beyond filthy. A real low point in my life. I have to applaud Debbie for sticking to her standards and not accepting that paid for week in a flophouse as severance. The Seton Hotel was awful.

Anyway, we were on an Amtrak train to visit the nutty bondage photographer couple I knew in Vermont. I had persuaded Debbie to get tied up and raped with me. She seemed happy enough at the prospect of a hundred and fifty bucks or so, and very cheerful about the overnight trip out of New York with little me. I really felt like the honey to the fly. She was sure about to get stuck real good. I didn't even get a commission for bringing her, as I recall. I think my motivation was that if they had another girl I'd still get my hundred fifty and they would focus on abusing her and I'd have an easier time of things. I'm sorry, Debbie.

She did her best to hustle beers for us on the trip up to Vermont on the Amtrak train, but we had to buy for ourselves.

The fish were nibbling, but there were no bites — she flirted and chatted with male passengers, and they seemed interested in us but not willing to buy us drinks. At one point, she asked me to join her in the crapper while she tried to shit. For about an hour, we were in there in the Amtrak toilet, drinking beer and chatting and taking sips of peppermint schnapps from the little bottle. The schnapps and beer were a rather nice high, actually, especially with the movement of the train. Her black jeans were down and she grimaced and tried to move her bowels.

Sure enough, she was bound, photographed and raped by the couple in Vermont. And I led her to the slaughter. At least I didn't have to be in the same room while she was raped. The husband tied me up and raped me, then went to play with Debbie, in another part of the rented farmhouse. She was just quiet about it all, afterwards. I guess she'd been raped before. I certainly had. Oh, on the train ride to Vermont, a cool looking young brunette chick stopped us to ask who we were. "We're bondage models on our way to a job," we proudly replied. Turns out she was in a punk chick group, The Delta Five. She was travelling to meet her group in Boston or something. We answered all her many questions and told us we lived wild and free, turned tricks, and got tied up and photographed from time to time to earn pin money. (Needle money, in Debbie's case.) About two hours later, she saw us again on the train and told us she'd written song lyrics about us, called "Bondage Babies" I never found out if the song was recorded or not, but Debbie and I dug it a lot, hearing this chick reciting her song lyrics to us on that train that day so long ago.

I lost track of Debbie over the next few months. My letters to her were returned unopened. One evening, however, I was crossing First Avenue and I saw Debbie, in her red leather jacket, with some guy — it may have been Johnny Thunders. We paused right in the middle of First Avenue, chatting as traffic rushed past us. She told me she was okay, but was spare on details. As we parted, she hugged me a little, and called me "girlfriend."

I had a birthday party for myself at the Plaza Hotel in June, 1981, just before I left for a semester of art school at the University of Florence. Debbie came to my party. She showed up late, and although I had been mugged that day and my face was bruised and all my party money had been taken, she persuaded me to order up from room service the cheapest dish they had for late night snacks: Welsh Rarebit. She slept in the same hotel bed with me and my boyfriend Henry, and Henry seemed very turned on and tickled by the situation, although I don't think he pulled her. She was all cheerful in the morning and let us, off to score and turn tricks, I guess.

One night at work at Katherine's, Debbie showed up moaning, "I o.d.'d last night! I always do two bags, but last night it was too much! My friends saved me!" I was horrified and so were the other relatively straight whores who worked there at Katherine's. (Katherine was in a New Age cult called Shariva and kept trying to get us to pay big bucks to go away for retreat weekends where we'd be purified and elevated. I wanted no part of that.) I feel sad when I remember Debbie. I wish I knew whatever became of her.

25. *Peeling Away At The Onion*

One of my pen pals, a prisoner in Great Britain, once remarked that I was like the proverbial onion — he suspected that if he kept peeling away all my layers, he'd just go on and on finding different sections of me. (Actually, I feel that way about HIM, but that's another story...) Anyway, I'd never heard that expression before, "peeling away at the onion."

Of course, I've forgotten a good many bondage modeling clients, and have no photographic proof of our encounters to share with you. But many of them were clients for years, and many of them continue to stay in touch. Eli was a really interesting case. He was mostly interested in being tied up himself, and figured a bondage model might give him a better session than a more ordinary type of dominatrix. He did like to take photos of me, and have me take photos of him. I don't have any examples of the photos he took of me, and the only one I have taken of him, I couldn't show you, because his face is not covered and he is too easily identifiable.

Eli was born and raised on Cape Cod, New England, and his full legal name suggests his family was Catholic. He owns several businesses on the Cape. I wouldn't call him rich, but he does all right. What happened to Eli is scary and could happen to you. His business sometimes took him to Brooklyn, where I lived. We tried to hook up there, but never managed it. Finally, he invited me to Boston, where he'd take me to dinner and then to his cottage on the Cape to spend the night. He forwarded no money or train tickets. As was often the case with me, if someone's letters seemed all right, I'd front the money and travel, sometimes great distances, to meet them for a session. People were generally so impressed I'd trusted them sufficiently to take that sort of risk on my own, they tended to be very generous and kind to me. I've only been stiffed out of money a few times in my modeling. One couple (the bondage photographers in Vermont) bounced checks on me at least once, and another couple flatly refused to pay me the amount they'd previously agreed upon at the end of a very long day's and a hard night's work. I cried very bitter tears, and of course never worked for them again, but there really wasn't much I could do to get back at them. (My sad story spread quickly among the little porn/kind community I ran in, and I found out later someone took revenge on them with me in mind, stealing several reels of undeveloped film footage they'd shot the day I was ripped off. Revenge!)

I got on an Amtrak train up to Boston to meet Eli. This was probably in 1979, but I'm very hazy on dates. I didn't even have the cash in hand to buy a return train ticket if Eli wasn't there, so I took a cab to the Avenue Victor Hugo bookshop, which sold my 'zine, BIKINI GIRL, and they said they were glad to see me and in fact owed me some money for some copies they'd sold. While they were paying me, I looked around the store, which had both new and used books as well as small press items for sale, and way up high, I spotted two or three very large, old and strange-looking books. I asked the clerk to climb a ladder and fetch them down for me. They seemed to be books on the magickal arts. "The Sacred Magic of Abra-Melin the Mage" was one of them. Another was a book of seals and letter formations. A third was a very general book on the supernatural. The publisher was de Laurence and I saw the name MacGregor Mathers. "How much for these books?" I asked the clerk. He got nervous.

"The people we got those books from are dead now, and it wasn't pretty. You really don't need to go messing with that stuff."

"How much?"

"Ten dollars."

I got all the books for a mere ten dollars, and had money left over from my 'zine sales. I thanked the scared-looking clerk, and got a cab over to the restaurant where I was to meet Eli.

The place was called The Magic Pan and featured crepes. I think it was in Faneuil Hall in Boston. He seemed to think it was a pretty impressive place for a first date, but to me, a crepe is just a pancake. We had a nice meal, however, and a couple of martinis relaxed me. Then we went to his car and he drove me for an hour or so into the pitch-black, late Autumn, barren Cape. I have no idea where the cottage was we stayed in that night. It was very dark when we arrived. I looked around the cottage while he unpacked my things and turned on some lights. It was a small but comfortable, plainly furnished little house. I immediately told him to strip and to kneel before me, while I put a slave collar on him. From that point on, he was to address me as "Mistress", and I was to address him as "slave." He was quiet and obedient.

Since bondage was to be the theme of the evening, I tied him up several different ways and left him on couches, beds or the floors while I read my new magick books, one of which was so scary I could feel my neck hairs prickle. Then, it got very late, so I untied him and we went to bed. He was very pleased with the session. I don't actually recall being paid anything for it, but I had my train fare and taxis reimbursed, I was fed dinner, drinks and breakfast, and I think he also gave me money for the magick books. Quite a few photos were taken, most of which I never saw again. Most were photos of him in bondage, but some were of me, as his bondage Mistress.

He took out a series of contact sheets and showed me his last long-term Mistress. She had white skin, long brown hair, and a very lush, dark bush of pubic hair. She posed for him in the various sexy leather outfits he'd bought her. They'd seen each other for quite a long time, but for one reason or another, had broken up. Eli was married and had a son, but very little was said about that. I wondered aloud how he could run around and have Mistresses on the side as he did, and he explained Cape Cod is a long distance to travel by car, and his business interests were scattered all over it. One of the reasons the family kept the cottage was that it was in between two of their businesses, and if he had to work late and got too tired, he could phone his wife and tell her he was going to crash there for the night. There was a phone in the cottage, of course, so the wife could call and check up on him if she needed to, but seemed to cut him a lot of slack. The wife had a full-time job in the health profession (I think she was a nurse), and her spare time was devoted to keeping the house in order and the son looked after. If her husband was gone for a day or two and do inventory at one of his businesses, she saw nothing odd about that. Nice little hard-working American family. Except that Eli, the husband, was out hiring bondage models like myself for little overnight flings.

Theirs was a family with a dirty little secret — a pile of naughty photographs, hidden in the trunk of one of Eli's cars. One day Eli got into a terrible car crash, and spent about six months in a coma in a hospital. His prognosis was not good. When the wife snapped out of it, she began looking through the papers in his home office, trying to find his life insurance policy, which it seemed she'd soon have to use. And there, in the back of one of his filing cabinets, was all the evidence: letters, photos, addresses and telephone numbers of Eli's little kink harem. He'd been answering personals ads and romping around with sluts like myself. Only when Eli was fully recovered and back running his businesses did the wife sit him down and explain to him why she wanted a divorce. He granted it, the property was fairly divided, and custody of the son was worked out. We were driving through North Truro when he told me this. "So, that's why I didn't hear from you for three years!" I murmured.

"Yup," he replied in his Yankee accent. "And to this day, I still don't remember the car accident! They say I never will."

"My God," was all I could say for the next several minutes. "Well, I'm glad you're okay now and we're together again." He smiled. He'd sent me airline tickets to fly from New York to Provincetown, where he'd rented us a very cute cottage for a couple of nights. Now that the community knew he was divorced, we could go out on regular dates together, me posing as just an ordinary girlfriend of his. We had some very fine meals, and there is a wonderful old bar out on a pier in Provincetown where you can suck down beer and hear terrific live music. "Put your arm around me. Be a little more affectionate," I heard Eli quietly say to me. I did so. "There's a woman at the bar who's glaring at us. I went out with her all last Summer and she dumped me and said I was a bore." I laughed very loudly.

"If only she knew all the interesting little hobbies you have!" He grinned and we had a good little laugh over that one. The straight ex-girlfriend continued to glare at him. If only she knew what he was really like, I thought to myself. Maybe she'd be less interested in staring him down in the bar.

I continued to fly to the Cape every Summer for long weekends with Eli for quite a few years. Eli always rented cute, clean, comfy little cottages for us on private beaches, and the best part was, he'd leave me alone for most of the day, while he went and checked on his businesses. I'd sunbathe and stroll along the beach and swim a little. He'd come back at the end of the day, go for a dip in the water with me, and then we'd shower and dress for cocktails and dinner. We'd take as long as we liked to eat and drink. What was the hurry? Back in our cottage, the implements of torture and a Polaroid camera were neatly stored away in laundry sacks tucked under the bed. We'd get back in quite late, and he'd slowly fill the ice bucket and fix me a nightcap. I'd turn on the TV and watch for awhile, while slowly dressing up in stockings, high heels, and some slutty little outfit, to arouse us both. Eli would kneel and strip down, and after the slave collar was on him, on went the nipple clamps, the testicle weights, the chains, etc. He'd be made to confess some sin, then be spanked or whipped for it, then made to kneel in the corner and think about his transgressions, while I sipped cocktails and watched TV. Finally, he was as hard as he could manage to be (he wasn't very well-endowed, poor Eli) so in order to jerk him off I'd make him kneel in front of me and I'd poke and prod my high heels into his penis and balls, until he'd squirt. He'd begin moaning, then would close his eyes and ejaculate on the carpeting.

Throughout the evening, he would ask me to stop to take various photos of me. This is what made our encounters about 90 percent me-dominant, but about ten percent him-dominant. He said he couldn't get a lot of Mistresses to give in and pose for him, but since I was a bondage model and used to the camera, I never seemed to mind, whereas sometimes the other women he cavorted with balked at being photographed. We got along well, me and Eli. I was never paid by Eli except to have nice weekends on Cape Cod, all paid for. We're still in touch.

One summer, Eli called me and complained he couldn't find reliable, honest sales help to work in one of his Cape Cod businesses. An old friend's brother, college age, newly come out as queer, leaped at the chance for a summer job in Provincetown, and ended up working for Eli for two or three years during tourist season. When I met and married my second husband, I used to take him to the very same seaside motel complex in Truro I'd once enjoyed so thoroughly with Eli. It's called the Seaside Village. Tell 'em Lisa sent you!

I had several slaves who were like Eli — not completely submissive. Sometimes (but very rarely!) we'd play "switch" and I'd get tied up, spanked, fucked, whatever. These were the riskiest sessions of all, I think. Once you begin reversing roles and mixing things up, misunderstandings can take place — and often do. I have one slave I like so much, we have not only decided we shall be friends for life, but that if circumstances allow it, we'll take romantic vacations together (probably camping and fishing — we both love to fish) and try to allow ourselves to fall in love and have a "real" relationship. So far, this guy has always been the slave in our games, but we've agreed that when I feel good and ready, I am going to switch and be the submissive. I warned him I'll probably fall in love with him very seriously then, so this is something we haven't tried yet. Also, we live on different continents and I'm remarried again! Oh, well. Always nice to know there's something brewing on a back burner.

By the way, in case you care to know, I've also worked as a "regular" model, it just didn't interest me much. There was a successful professional photographer with a nice studio in SoHo and, by his accounts, a cozy bachelor pad up in Westchester I never was invited to see. I don't think I ever had sex with this guy, or even went out for a drink or food with him. It was all modeling work. His specialty was cookbook covers. He photographed very everyday, boring things, and made them look lovely on the cover, so the book would sell. He also did quite a few romance novel covers. Now, you and I both know, romance fiction usually has artwork on the cover, and not a photo, but you probably didn't know that cover artwork is often copied and developed from a photograph, first. I'd pose in flimsy gowns, falling off my shoulders and showing my meager cleavage, and thrust out a sandal-clad leg, standing on a rock in a studio, a fan blowing at my long dark blonde hair. Sometimes there were shackles around my ankles or some other dramatic effect. This work paid very little and took a lot of time and patience, but it made for a nice change of pace. A real makeup artist was always hired, and I loved watching while he or she painted a new mask over my plain features, curled and coaxed my long, fine hair into place with pins, tied it with ribbons, and led me to the studio, where I'd have to pose this way and that for one or two hours, not knowing at all the nature of the project. I was usually offered a shower to get all the makeup and hairspray off me (and some of the studio dirt), then was paid in cash or an always-good check, and off I went.

Of course, photographers hired me often merely in exchange for a nice print of myself. Barter. When I was 18 and 19 years old and an art student in Kent, Ohio, I earned money on the side by working as an artists' model for the art department. It paid minimum wage and the studios were usually cold. (Winters are severe in Ohio.) Striking poses for a room of life drawing students wasn't very interesting, but it was, in my mind, honest work. The first time I stepped out nude was quite a rush! All those eyes upon me! But I could see right away that although a few students would always rudely ogle me, most of them were just there to draw and were grateful to get a model who could change poses quickly and then hold still as long as needed.

At this time I learned to steal the fruits and vegetables set out for still life paintings. If I could get a leek and several potatoes, I could steal some butter pats and salt and pepper packets from the cafeteria. I'd have to buy only a tiny quantity of cheap flour. I learned to melt the butter in a pan over a hotplate, slowly stir in the flour, salt and pepper until it became light brown, then add the chopped, heavily rinsed leek and the potatoes and add several cups of water. An hour or two later I had a fine soup, more than enough to share with my roomies who, like me, always seemed hungry. I guess people call these "salad days." Hungry times, when you'll go and steal the food from art department still life setups, to get your dinner.

When I was with the Dorothy Palmer Talent Agency in New York, I was sent out to pose one night for a "real" artist who was taking large photographs in black and white of naked white women who wore strange masks and lunged at each other with dildoes. I told one of the models I had been offered to go visit the couple in

Vermont. "Don't go!" she begged me. "They're really weird!" But of course — as you know — I went anyway. She had just been to see them. "They're weird," she repeated, "and the guy raped me."

My first husband was a fashion photographer, and specialized in catalogue work. Sometimes I'd help him out by posing for him so he could get the lighting right, or even helping out as a stylist when he needed me. But he didn't work much — he wanted to play — and the marriage was over in a few months, anyway. He was into drugs, and the hardcore New York S/M scene. I walked out on him one night, never to return.

Of the many who have written to me, there are some very, very sad cases. The ones I'd rather not think much about. One guy, Eddie from Staten Island, was a gravedigger. It was a Union job, he explained, and he enjoyed it, but said it gave him a hard time in getting dates. I told him I thought it was an important and respectable job and as long as he dug the best graves he possibly could, I respected him for that. Eddie was very shy. He wanted to be my slave but also sent out plenty of signals that he expected me to dance to his various demented tunes. I decided that it would be his job to bring me a bottle of Corvo white wine every Saturday, and take away a pair of my shoes and have them repaired. While he was out, I'd drink about half the bottle of wine and listen to records. I'd chill a nice glass for him, and pour some wine into it, adding a generous dollop of my urine. He'd come back with the shoes repaired, and I'd watch him drink his glass of wine.

He asked if he could buy me shoes and if I would model them for him in the little East Village apartment I shared. I said yes, I would. He brought me a pair with impossibly high heels, and I put on pink stockings with a garter belt and wore them for him for an hour or two. He seemed very pleased, and went away. But many months later, he came back and said he couldn't see me anymore, because I was too nice — too reasonable — too cooperative. I don't think he knew at all what he really wanted. And I wonder how he would have felt about me knowing he drank some of my piss each time he visited.

Gary wanted to set me up as his little Downtown Mistress. I don't recall how we met, but it was probably through a personals ad. He had quite a standard range of fantasies. I am including him in this chapter because, once again, it is not entirely clear to me who was the dominant and who was the submissive in this relationship. Ostensibly, he wanted to be the slave, but everything had to be his way, and most Mistresses wouldn't put up with that, of course. He liked me because he knew I could be both dominant and submissive. One of his fantasies was to be my chauffeur. He had a nice car. I instructed him to drive me to the Chelsea Hotel. I went upstairs and fucked a musician, then said my driver was waiting, excused myself, and left. Gary had waited, but it hadn't been a long visit. The musician was quick at the draw. That is to say, he came within a few minutes of penetration.

Gary's family was in the garment business. He came to pick me up one night and asked me if I was hungry and I said yes, very hungry, so he took me to the Village Arts coffee shop on Eighth Street. He never sprang for a nice restaurant with me, but what did I care? I ate club sandwiches and had bowls of matzoh ball soup while I listened to his spiel. What a bullshit artist Gary was! I asked them to refill the halfsour pickle tray and to get me another beer, while I listened to his latest speech. He didn't even know my name. He thought I was "Liz Jones" I liked it that way. I was curious about his Jewish, garment-industry family.

"Fancy garments?" I asked Gary, stuffing some tuna salad into my hungry mouth. "Aw, shit, no, Liz. My father, he always says, `Sell to the classes, eat with the masses. Sell to the masses, eat with the classes.' Naw, we do mostly cheap polyester house robes for shapeless female customers out in New Jersey. Inexpensive stuff, inexpensively produced. Moves like crazy. They can't get enough of that crap. And my family and I have a wonderful mansion in Lynbrook and belong to good clubs."

"Even though you're Jews?" I asked him, getting a refill on my seltzer with lemon. He winced.

"Yeah," he said quietly, his face darkening. Then, he brightened. "You know, Liz," he began, "I really like you. If I was to promise you a charm bracelet from a good jeweler, I wouldn't give you something second-class from a costume jeweler."

"You're very sweet, Gary," I replied. "I like you, too." I knew I'd never see any type of jewelry off this guy. I sure never did.

"How'd you like to visit my family's house with me tonight?" They're away. I want you to tie me up on my bed and whip my ass."

"Okay," I said.

So we got into his very fancy car, a Jaguar or something, and he drove me out to Long Island and sure enough, the family house (on a small but neatly kept lot) was quiet. He offered me a drink and gave me cheese bits on a plate, which I promptly wolfed down, knowing I'd have no dinner that night. He then led me to his bedroom. All very clean. There was at least one maid employed by his family, all the carpeting was plush and wall-to-wall. His parents had matching movable beds so they could sit up and watch TV. Gary's bed had a big fancy comforter on it, and he took out a collection of his neckties, stripped, and face down, I tied him to his bed posts and whipped his large ass. "Oh, Liz, Oh, Liz," he moaned. When it was over, he drove me back to the East Village. I fell asleep on the way. He got me home safely. I gave him the lining from one of my raincoats to have dry cleaned. I didn't hear from him for six months, so assumed the lining was lost, and cursed myself. Miraculously, I got the ticket stub mailed to me later that year, and rushed to pick up my coat lining, which hadn't even been paid for.

Gary called again — he'd gotten a nice apartment on the Upper East Side. Would I like to see him? I said I was too busy.

26. *Diary Entry*

Late November, 1979, New York City

I saw "Scorpio Rising" this week and can't get motorcycle fantasies out of my head. A big, Caucasian guy, clean-shaven, huge, hard chest (blond hair). All in black leather gear. No shirt under his open jacket. I kneel. He is yanking me down by my hair. His cock comes out and it's in my mouth. I deep throat it and a thick slime saliva caresses it — a rigid, curved shaft with sweet pre-come seasoning tip. He throws me to the floor, kicks my legs open, stands there high and inspects. He mounts me, his eyes peering cruelly into mine. I look away. He jerks my head back, forces me into his gaze. His lips and mouth are so perfect and hard.

Oh, God, he is heavy! He pins my shoulders and arms easily. He is so big. He pierces me all in one move, no preliminary test-thrust. The lips violate mine, the tongue is sweet and oh, I try to caress him but my arms are pinned. And just as I start to lapse into unconsciousness, the pounding reminds me, and I look up. There he is, raping me.

It goes for so long. I have come in dizzy tornadoes so many times, but my cunt is wet and his attack is left undefended.

He lies flat upon me, his chest hard, his gorgeous neck arched, and squeezes my shoulders, almost a hug, but I hear his tiny high grunts and I know he is oblivious to me. His cock twitches and I feel it grow, the thrusts so fast and easy and forceful, his balls tapping me gently in the ass every move in. "Uh-uh-uh," he moans softly, and my eyes roll back, every muscle in me vibrates, I see sparks, long shoots of light, and I'm falling 10,000 feet, dizzy from the slow-motion spin, but he holds me with his huge bulging arms and I'm not afraid.

"Oh, I love you," I whisper, or did I just think it to myself?

And YANK! Hot come shoots straight deep into me, and he pushes, one, two, THREE, then rests, breathing hard.

He sat in the black vinyl chair and leaned back, relaxing. Even reclining, his muscles arched, luscious tight curves and flat, angular planes. He wore only those tight, tight pants — his legs were long, and they spread as men's legs do. The bulge in his crotch was large, but not obscene. I envisioned the stiff upright rod being pressed close to his flat belly by the tight-fitting trousers. His face was frightening, stern, his expression calculating and malevolent.

The personality I had known so well in him was replaced with that of an all-powerful, magnificent stranger. I stood gaping, self-conscious, but transfixed.

"Open your blouse," he said. I did so quickly, my nervous fingers shaking a little, nearly tearing the button-holes. "Let it fall."

It slid off my shoulders, down my back, past my wrists, and I felt myself blush, my small but shapely breasts pushed up cutely by a little black lace underwire bra. "That goes next," he said, and I unsnapped it in back, blushing redder, unable to look into his eyes. "That skirt — drop it." I dared not hesitate. It slipped down and I stepped out of it, shivering, although no draft invaded the dimly lit room. "And the panties. NOW!" When these were tossed away, I was naked and vulnerable, clad only in black, thigh-high elastic-top stockings, and spike-heeled opera pumps of black, shiny leather.

He was not moving.

"Lie down," he said. "On your back, bitch." The floor was cold. Why was I obeying so blindly? I couldn't see him now. Shadows streaked the ceiling. My nipples stood erect. I longed to touch them, to relieve them, but dared not move.

I winced at the next command. "Spread them. WIDE." And he must have sat there for ages, inspecting me.

Finally, I heard him rise.

"Now, tell me what I am doing to you," he said evenly, coldly.

"Y-you are making me lie here, open, waiting for you."

"Waiting for what?" He stood perfectly still, and I began to grow tense with fear.

"For your cock," I whispered, my voice growing hoarse, my breaths becoming strange and short.

"That's right," he sneered. "Now tell me why you're waiting for my cock."

"Because I'm yours," I gasped. "Because I want your cock in me."

SLAP! He had reached down to strike my face, and my skin burned, my senses reeling. My deep breaths turned to tiny sobs, hot tears of frustration stinging my cheeks. "Yes, you're mine," he corrected. "But you're waiting for my cock because I want to rape you."

My whimpers sounded piteous, animal-like, but I couldn't control myself. He offered no consolation, and I had to choke those whimpers down until they eventually subsided. A new energy was building in me, a new yearning.

I heard the snap of his leather belt, the jingle of the buckle, and the zipper that encased the growing bulge. I closed my eyes tight, the sounds he made while moving around the room becoming meaningless, endless, timeless. His large hand caught my wrists easily, and I felt a thick, stretchy cord wrapped quickly around them. The knot jerked to a rigid lump between my palms when he pulled, and my arms were yanked above my head. I think he tied the other end of the cord to a pipe near the wall.

This bondage, deceptively light, had me flat on my back, without the use of my arms. To rise would have meant an awkward fish flop, but never could I free myself before he would be on top of me, holding me down with his enormous frame. As he mounted me, I resisted with my thighs, and he jerked my chin to his face, squeezing until I looked him in the eyes, and his eyes were awesome — piercing, narrow slits, the former ice-blue now a grim pale gray, his expression so cold and detached it alarmed me, actually terrified me to the core. No traces of familiarity, even recognition of my person, existed in the cruel mask he was wearing. My resistance gave way to humble submission, a crawly moist sensation pulsating between my legs. I drew breath deeply, and felt myself float.

The stiff, curving rod shoved into me, my cunt involuntarily tight, the pain terrific. He gave me no chance to open, to relax and allow entry a bit at a time. The cold, hard belt buckle jabbed me repeatedly. I started to protest, but his mouth pressed over mine, his tongue violating me, suppressing my cries.

The cords at my wrists held fast, growing tighter if I struggled, and a pain was forming all over, causing my back to arch, my legs to kick the air uselessly, my spiked heels jabbing nothingness in rhythmic jerks.

Stars and galaxies spun inside my head, and no sound reached my ears but his steady breathing. His scent was strong, and dizzying, and I was being spent while he was barely exerting himself.

I recently came across this piece of writing while looking through one of my old diaries. I have kept journals, diaries and sketchbooks since early childhood. Upon re-reading it, I realize that most of it actually happened to me with a boyfriend I had at that time.

I've worked on this book for a year and a half now. I'm surprised it has taken me so long to eke out these few chapters. Remembering my bondage modeling past has dredged up a lot of strange memories and emotions. I wonder why people engage in self-destructive behavior? When you stand back and look at it, of course it seems utterly stupid. Why do people willingly harm and degrade themselves? If you want to suffer, it seems more reasonable, certainly more admirable, to engage in charity work. I mean, go and care for lepers and/or live like Mother Theresa if you need to do stuff like that, suffering and all. But no, instead, we sit in front of porn videos, beat off, and do lines. Are we inherently weak, evil and lazy? I am not sure about the answer to that. I have as many positive impulses as I have negative ones.

I like the theory put forth by William Peter Blatty in his book, "Legion." He says that Lucifer was the much-beloved of God, but sought to exist. In doing so, it was necessary to break away from God, to enter the realm of material existence. God allowed Lucifer to break away the way a loving parent allows his or her child to go off and play in the streets, knowing well it is likely the child will be harmed. Yet, the child longs to run and play, so the parent must let go out of love. The parent hopes the child will return one day, mature and whole. Lucifer, in the very act of existing, brought forth this physical world we live in. He is the light-bearer. "Let there be light." But in leaving God, he destroyed himself. He fell. Never fell out of favor with God, never lost God's love. But like Adam and Eve, Lucifer left the perfect garden and sought to live on this earthly plane. The ultimate self-destructive act. And Lucifer broke into a hundred hundred million pieces. Since he was the beloved of God, each particle was perfection, and went toward creating the diverse and gorgeous and monstrous world in which we live. Some religions believe that the world was not created by God, but created by a "deputy."

Just as Lucifer broke into pieces, he naturally wants to be whole again, and reunited with God. So that is why we, who are but tiny fragments of Lucifer, feel deep in our hearts the desire to be one with God again. And that is why there is at the same time such beauty and perfection on Earth as there is at the same time such horror and evil. Of my own failings, weaknesses and foibles I am all too aware. Am I a good person? Am I a dirty whore? And what makes a whore dirty? That she peddles her own body, or allows it to be sold by another? What could, in fact, be more human? But are "human" things inherently bad? Matters of the flesh.

They say flesh is weak. I know mine is. When I got this publisher to agree to publish my recollections about being a bondage model, I was at first ecstatic. I've known plenty of whores but also a few bondage models. A whore who writes is nothing new. But I wanted to be the bondage model who spoke up about my specialization. That is why I have written this book. Many times in the past, bondage models as well as customers have said to me, "Lisa, you have to write about this some day." I promised most of them I would.

Most of the bondage models I knew are either dead or have tired and don't want to think about what they did and don't want to speak up about it. I am sort of a crusader, and that is essentially so cheap. What the hell do I think I am crusading for? I stupidly thought I'd derive some feeling of satisfaction or even titillation by writing these sleazy memoirs. Instead, I have only given myself more pain. I have had to stand in front of myself and look at all the ugly parts and pieces of which I am made. It has been difficult, also, to write about the men and women who hired me to be tied up and have my pictures taken

Part of the time, I was of course involved in their sexual experiences, but other times, I was just a commodity to be bought, sold and exploited. Unfortunately, I usually thought I was in control. They say the submissives are the ones who are truly manipulating the scene. I used to believe that, but now, I am not so sure of it. I've said it before and I'll say it again: most of the people I've known in prostitution were average people who were just trying to put food on the tables of their families. The drug addicts, alcoholics, and nut cases were the exception to the twisted rule. Okay, most of 'em had some seriously damaged parts and sad histories: childhood abuse, rape, general deprivation. So, basically, I don't know what the fuck I am talking about.

Finally, I hope you have enjoyed reading this, and that it has provoked you to think about a great many things. Writing it has been painful. I am not proud of what I've done.

I WAS FOR SALE.